Korean FTA: Policy and Law

KOREAN FTA POLICY AND LAW

BONGCHUL KIM · HO KIM
JOONPYO LEE · HYELIM LEE

HU:iNE

Korean FTA : Policy and Law

by *Bongchul Kim, Ho Kim, Joonpyo Lee, Hyelim Lee*

First published 01 September, 2015

Published by HANKUK UNIVERSITY OF FOREIGN STUDIES KNOWLEDGE PRESS
107, Imun-ro, Dongdaemun-gu, Seoul 02450, Korea
Tel. 82-2-2173~2497, Fax. 82-2-2173-3363

E-mail press@hufs.ac.kr

Online http://press.hufs.ac.kr

Design EwhanD&B T. 82-2-2254-4301

Print SM C&P T. 82-2-468-6100

ISBN 978-89-7464-839-8 93320

Price 11,000 Won

Preface

Preface

The reasons of rapid increase for Regional or Preferential Trade Agreements (RTAs or PTAs) in the international Economic and Trade related stage are promotion of trade and enhancement of bargaining power. Korea has joined many types of multilateral international agreements and also made several Free Trade Agreements (FTAs) with its major economic partners. The Korean government thought that RTAs could be an effective way to respond actively to the new trend of Regionalism in late 1990s. Since then, the government has continued to promote its FTA policy and improved the related laws.

Korea, a small nation in Asia, has been overcoming the difficulties of post-war circumstances and has shown the remarkable economic development and cultural sophistication in half a century. The Korean government has been trying to establish its own sets of international economic systems since 2000 as a member of the international society. As time has passed, there have been numerous attempts to cultivate the 'Korean Style,' which is based on Korea's experiences in the field of Economic Development. Regardless of various endeavors, FTA related policies and laws; Korea still has many challenges to overcome.

This book explains the basic concept of policies, systems, and laws regarding Korean FTAs, and introduces cases that identify problems and proposes the future tasks. Each author focuses on detailed explanations of Korean FTAs, recognizes challenges of certain fields, and organized those in an orderly manner to assist further comprehension. This book deals with the Korean FTAs, which are receiving the international attention, in English and gives a comprehensive view of the problems at hand. Thus, this book is initially, a general introductive book for the undergraduates who have learned the basic concepts of the FTAs for the first time. Secondly, it is a lecture material for those who has shown constant attention in Korean FTAs.

The authors of this book are the young intellectuals who have been studying the Korean FTA issues. They have been discussing over Korean FTA as mentors, mentees and colleagues for a long time. These concerns are still present matters and will continue to be in the future. Therefore, there might be mistakes and errors in this particular literature, and it will still be a challenge to be improved as the current Korean FTA.

Editor
Bongchul Kim

Contents

Chapter 1.
The Legal Aspects of the possible CJK FTA

The Legal Aspects of the possible CJK FTA

Bongchul Kim

I. Introduction

The international economic policies of the countries in the Northeast Asian region have been mainly focused on the RTAs (Regional Trade Agreements) or PTAs (Preferential Trade Agreements) in recent years. The three countries (China, Japan and Korea) in this emerging economically and aggressively changing region have agreed that they need to have their RTA and they are now considering the Northeast Asian or CJK FTA (China-Japan-Korea Free Trade Agreement).

They have agreed that the CJK FTA will be beneficial to the

region and to each country based on a considerable number of joint research. Although there are still several obstacles to reach the goal, the three countries have already put the importance of this FTA in their RTA policy for the future. Many specialists on this issue have proposed several ways to reach the goal.

In the part of the law, the concept of the FTA is interesting. It is a type of RTAs and useful and important as a legal tool for international trade and economy. Therefore, legal researches are needed for the possible CJK FTA to make the centre point of international economic law in this region. The main objective of this chapter is to research the legal issues surrounding the possible CJK FTA. This topic will be important when they start designing the articles of the FTA and improving domestic laws of the members.

II. The Northeast Asian Regionalism and the CJK FTA

1. The Regionalism in the Northeast Asian Region

Northeast Asia has been drawing increasing attention from the international community because of the region's dynamic economic power and strategic value. The two axes of the circle are China and Japan, and Korea is located between the two countries from the geopolitical perspective of the region. The region's economic power and strategic value from geoeconomic perspectives are namely, China's growing economy and its potential, Japan's massive capital and technology, Korea's post crisis economic recovery and dynamism, which have brought a new dimension to the globalising world of the twenty-first century.

- The RTA policy of China

After the WTO accession in 2000, China is one of the major players in the world trade and economy. This situation presents both opportunities and challenges for the world economy as well as the neighbouring countries in the Northeast Asian region.[1)]

China pushed its RTA policy after it became a member of the WTO. It is committed to accomplishing the following strategic objectives through implementing RTAs: to create stable relations with neighbouring countries; to explore new markets to avoid the troubles of MTAs; to provide the critical strategic resources required for to economic development; to push Chinese enterprises 'to go abroad' on the RTA platform; to enhance the overall competitiveness of domestic industries via reasonable competition, and to resolve the issues of its market economy status with RTAs.[2)]

China has signed so far Closer Economic Partnership Agreements (CEPAs) with Hong Kong and Macao, FTAs with many other countries such as Chile, Pakistan, and ASEAN. Chinese counterpart nations include a wider range of countries around the world. This shows that China is using the RTA as a worldwide mean of international politics. It seems that one of the Chinese goals for RTAs is to build its position as a leading nation in world politics.[3)]

The roadmap presented by the Chinese government in 2005 indicates the major goals of China's RTA policy. First, China plans to play a leading role in building an East Asian Economic Integration Body. China wants to develop a China-oriented economic cooperation structure in the region with the China-ASEAN FTA and the CEPAs with Hong Kong and Macao.

Furthermore, the Chinese leadership in this region could fulfil China's other objectives involving security and the resolution of disputes with its neighbours in the region. This is also important to China as it is in competition with Japan of the region.[4)]

Second, promotion of the Northeast Asian RTA or CJK FTA will benefit the development of the Northeast Asian region and China. Third, China plans to secure stable supply of resources and energy. Since China is experiencing a shortage of energy due to its uncontrollable growth, energy security is one of China's major national agendas.

Fourth, China is expecting the expansion of its market share around the world with RTA relations. Chinese competitiveness would allow its international market share to expand as a result of the RTA. Lastly, China seems to be planning a path to major hegemony against the United States using RTA policy. The diversity of RTA counterparts around the world indicates the importance of non-economic factors in Chinese RTA policy making.[5)]

- The RTA policy of Japan

Japanese government officials took the multilateral liberalisation process more seriously and disregarded the shifting trend to Regionalism before the Asian crisis in the 1990s. However, the difficulties of WTO negotiations and the RTA trend around the world stimulated Japan to take their RTA trade policy. Japan concluded an EPA with Singapore in November 2002 for the first time, and subsequently signed EPAs[6] with many countries including the ASEAN members such as Malaysia, Philippines, Thailand and Indonesia. In 2008, ASEAN and Japan signed on the comprehensive EPAs (AJCEP Agreement).

The characteristics of Japanese RTAs are threefold. Firstly, Japan has chosen ASEAN members as a priority in picking their RTA counterparts. Japan signed EPAs with ASEAN member countries individually, and finished as the AJCEP Agreement. Although the Japanese government is expecting that the AJCEP Agreement will maximise the economic benefit, this policy also intends to restrain rising Chinese influence in this region.

Secondly, Japan has sensitive agricultural and fishery sectors.[7] Therefore, Japan required effective exclusion or, at least, some form of special treatment regarding these sectors in many RTA negotiations. As a result of this, the level of Japanese market entry in the manufacturing sector is low, while that in agriculture and fishery is relatively high in its RTAs.

Thirdly, Japanese RTA policy shows non-economic factors are more important in their policy decision-making. Japan seeks to make a favourable international political environment in pursuing its goals in the international community. In particular, Japan intends to take a leading position in the economic community in the region of East Asia, competing with China. Curbing China's rise in Southeast Asia seems to be another important policy goal for Japan as is shown by RTAs with ASEAN countries. Japan's choice for an RTA counterpart shows its interest is overwhelmingly in developing countries, rather than developed countries.

- The RTA policy of Korea

Korea turned its eyes to RTAs after the Asian financial crisis in 1997. The crisis provided the momentum to promote Regionalism in Korea as one of the means to propel economic reform. The Korean government expected that RTAs can be the vehicles for their recovery from the economic and financial crisis with their systemic reforms including their domestic laws.

Two major reasons can be suggested for the change of the policy. First, Korea started RTA negotiations to minimise damage to its trade as Regionalism spread around the world after the launch of the EU in 1992 and NAFTA in 1994. Korea wanted to avoid remaining as an outsider in the worldwide trend. It took the RTA policy to maintain its market and move into a new market at the same time. The second goal of its RTA policy was to strengthen economic competitiveness and improve its national economic system through the opening of its market and liberalisation. Korea intended to utilise RTAs in promoting qualitative growth of the Korean economy and leaping into a more advanced economy. In fact, they have improved many types of rules and regulations following the international standards after the policy.

Korea has four strategies in pursuing RTAs with other countries. First, it pursues simultaneous RTA negotiations with interested counterpart countries. This is to overcome the delay in RTA competitiveness over the last 15 years and thereby to minimise the cost generated by Korean companies and eventually by the Korean economy. Second, Korea seeks a comprehensive RTA in terms of coverage and content. Its agenda includes trade in goods, trade in services, investment, government procurement, technical barriers and intellectual property, in order to attain a higher level of RTAs which would make up for multilateral liberalisation and help domestic economic reform. Third, the Korean government takes national consensus building and a transparent process as important factors to consider as it promotes RTAs. Fourth, Korea will drive RTAs with large economies such as the US, EU, ASEAN and India.

2. The close but tangled relations in the region

The three countries in the region reveal different characteristics in their RTAs. In selecting counterparts for their RTAs, China and Japan tend to pick developing countries while Korea tends to choose advanced countries such as EFTA and the US. These kinds of country choice patterns reflect the different goals of the three countries. Korea as a middle-ranking power in the world tends to emphasise economic benefit while China and Japan as major powers in the world tend to focus relatively more on non-economic values.

This relates to the next characteristic of RTA policies of the three countries. China and Japan seem to pursue regional hegemony in East Asia through RTA policies. Both countries took ASEAN member countries as important RTA counterparts and put higher priority on ASEAN in their RTA negotiations. ASEAN was the first FTA counterpart to China and the China-ASEAN FTA was signed in November 2004. Japan, on the other hand, put emphasis on individual FTAs with ASEAN member countries and signed FTAs with major ASEAN members. In the case of China, building a base for a world hegemonic nation competing with the United States seems to be a hidden goal of its RTA policies. On the other hand, Korea's interest as an FTA partner of ASEAN is more focused on economic benefit. Korea took its FTA initiative as a way to advance its economic system and revive from economic crisis.

In terms of fields of interest, China considers energy and resource security as one of the prime goals of RTAs around the world. Japan prefers a lower level of market entry in agriculture and fishery, while allowing high market entry in the manufacturing sector. Korea, meanwhile, pursues a comprehensive FTA including services, investment, government procurement, intellectual property rights, and so on.

The share of intraregional trade between China, Japan and Korea has risen substantially from 12.7% in 1990 to 23.9% in 2005. In 2006, Japan and Korea were the second and fourth largest trading partners, respectively, for China. For Japan, the second and third most important trading partners were China and Korea, respectively, after the United States. China and Japan were the first and second largest trading partners, respectively, for Korea.

3. The CJK FTA? – Several approaches to the Goal

In this situation, before and after the Asian financial crisis in 1997, there have been some attempts at economic cooperation in the region.[8)] Even though China, Korea and Japan were not ready to consider formal regional economic integration, they have become interested in the idea of forming a Northeast Asian FTA (CJK FTA). From a long term view, the CJK FTA can be regarded as the first step for the 'Northeast Asian Community' as the ultimate vision for Northeast Asian economic integration. The scholars and governments of the countries have discussed the subject and they have proposed several ways to achieve this goal.

First of all, the three countries can consider the trilateral negotiations for the CJK FTA.[9)] Although this will be the most direct way to the goal, it has many political or other obstacles for the countries to overcome at the same time.[10)] Secondly, they can take two steps for the goal as a second option.[11)] In other words, they may have bilateral FTAs between two countries of the region such as the China-Korea FTA as the first step, then, integrate their FTAs to the CJK FTA as the second step. In this method, three countries can also consider one bilateral FTA of two countries and the participation of the other country in the FTA. Lastly, at the broader regional level, the ASEAN+3 idea is discussing plans for an 'East Asian Community' as a new framework for Regionalism. This aims at strengthening and deepening East Asian cooperation and foresees the establishment of a region wide RTA. The three countries already have developed their FTA relations with ASEAN in different ways. Therefore, if they harmonise the FTAs, the ASEAN+3 FTA can be realised. This must be taken into account when thinking about the CJK FTA.[12)]

Although there may be controversy on the methods to achieve the goal, the three countries need to have the CJK FTA now. They have agreed that the CJK FTA will be a win-win-win strategy for the three countries, bringing benefits to them all. However, they still have many issues to discuss the CJK FTA in addition to political and emotional obstacles. There have been several joint studies of the three countries for these matters since 2003.[13)] The three countries should harmonise and overcome the differences for building the CJK FTA. The Northeast Asia of the CJK FTA is possible and should be realised in the near future.[14)]

III. The legal Frame of the CJK FTA

1. The RTA and FTA in the WTO system

The phenomenon of Regionalism is prominent in today's international trading system. Now, roughly more than one-half of world trade is performed under the preferential treatments of RTAs. Although the coverage and depth of preferential treatment varies from one RTA to another, the bases and concepts of RTAs can be contrasted against multilateral trade agreements.

The networks of RTAs are overlapping and their map is becoming more complicated with the proliferation of RTAs. Here, several issues are emerging regarding the linkages or the conflicts between RTAs and the WTO in different legal aspects. Excepting the case of RTAs to which one or more non-WTO member states are party, when a WTO member enters into an RTA through which it grants more favourable conditions to its trade with other WTO member parties to that agreement than to other WTO members' trade, it departs from the guiding principle of non-discrimination defined in Article I of GATT, Article II of GATS, and elsewhere. WTO Members are, however, permitted to enter into such RTAs under specific conditions, which are spelled out in three sets of rules:

- *Article XXIV of the GATT (as clarified in the Understanding on the Interpretation of Article XXIV of the GATT 1994) provides for the formation and operation of customs unions and FTA covering trade in goods.*
- *The so-called Enabling Clause (the 1979 Decision on Differential and More Favourable Treatment, Reciprocity and Fuller Participation of Developing Countries) refers to RTAs in trade in goods between developing countries.*
- *Article V of the GATS governs the conclusion of RTAs in the area of trade in services, for both developed and developing countries.*

The main provisions in Article XXIV of the GATT are as follows. First, the establishment of an RTA is acceptable under the GATT so long as its purpose is to facilitate trade within the region and not to raise barriers to trade with outside economies. Second, duties and other restrictive regulations of commerce shall not be on the whole higher or more restrictive than the corresponding duties and other regulations of commerce existing in the same constituent territories prior to the formation of the RTA. Third, duties and other restrictive regulations of commerce shall be eliminated on substantially all trade between the constituent territories in respect of products originating in such territories.[15)]

While an Understanding on the Interpretation of Article XXIV of the GATT 1994 was adopted as a part of the Uruguay Round Final Act, this Understanding by and large addresses technical issues that have surfaced in the application of Article XXIV and does not alter the fundamental approach of the GATT to customs unions and FTAs.[16)]

The official name of the Enabling Clause is 'the 1979 Decision on Differential and More Favourable Treatment, Reciprocity and Fuller Participation of Developing Countries.' This decision by signatories to the GATT in 1979 allows derogations to the MFN treatment in favour of developing countries. In particular, its paragraph 2(c) permits RTAs among developing countries in goods trade. It has continued to apply as part of GATT 1994 under the WTO, and is therefore still in force. It allows RTAs among developing country Members in derogation from the MFN treatment obligation of Article I of the GATT. The conditions that RTAs under the Enabling Clause must meet are less demanding and less specific than those set out in Article XXIV of the GATT.[17)] The Enabling Clause does not direct any specific forms of RTAs, so arguably any form of RTA might be permitted under this clause. The RTAs under the Enabling Clause include the AFTA by ASEAN members.

As a result of the GATS, the multilateral trade system does now, for the first time, deal with RTAs extending beyond trade in goods and covering the supply of services (and, indirectly, foreign direct investments and movement of workers). Article V of GATS is the counterpart of Article XXIV of GATT for trade in services. Article V:1(b) of the GATS requires that an RTA should provide for 'the absence or elimination of substantially all discrimination.' Furthermore, the footnote to the Article V requires that RTAs do have 'substantial coverage' in terms of number of sectors, volume of trade affected and modes of supply.

Article V bis, entitled 'Labour Markets Integration Agreements', deals with a specific form of RTA which establishes full integration of labour markets between or among the parties to such an agreement. Such agreements give the nationals of the parties' free entry to each other's labour markets. Usually, these agreements also include provisions concerning conditions of pay, other conditions of employment and social benefits. Article V bis provides that the GATT shall not prevent any WTO member from being a party to such agreement provided that the agreement exempts citizens of parties to the agreement from requirements concerning residency and work permits and is notified to the Council for Trade in Services.[18)]

A recent statistic of the WTO shows that most RTAs have been notified to the WTO after 1995. Some 462 RTAs have been notified to the GATT/WTO up to February 2010. 345 of these RTAs were notified under Article XXIV of the GATT 1947 or GATT 1994, 31 under the Enabling Clause, and 86 under Article V of the GATS. At that same date, 271 agreements were in force.

2. How can we design the provisions? – An example of the safeguard issue

Considering that RTAs affect each other and are also connected with WTO agreements, it is worth analysing the articles of RTAs and WTO rules on specific issues for designing new RTAs. For example, if an RTA provides different rules from the WTO rules in the trade remedy area such as safeguards, the first issue can be raised in relation to Article XXIV of the GATT.[19] However, even if the RTA provisions on the trade remedy area satisfy the conditions of Article XXIV, there are still other issues in this area. Sometimes the issues come from the imperfection of the WTO rules in the area.

Again, this may be one of the reasons for some RTAs to provide more detailed or different rules than the WTO. In particular, in the area of safeguards which is one of the most popular issues for international trade disputes in the stages of the WTO, this method is important for reducing the disputes between the parties of the RTA. Then, how can we design the articles on the safeguard measures in the CJK FTA? It may be an example for the construction of the whole provisions of the FTA.

- Safeguard measures in the WTO system

Safeguard measures are defined as emergency actions with respect to increased imports of particular products, where such imports have caused or threaten to cause serious injury to the importing country's domestic industry. Such measures can consist of quantitative import restrictions or of duty increases to higher than bound rates. They are one of three types of trade remedy measures, along with antidumping and countervailing measures, available to WTO Members.

The Agreement on Safeguards sets forth the rules for application of safeguard measures pursuant to Article XIX of GATT. Article XIX of GATT provides for an escape from the obligations otherwise imposed by GATT when it can be demonstrated that imports increased either absolutely or relative to domestic production causing serious injury or threat of serious injury to domestic producers and that the increase occurred as a result of unforeseen developments and as a result of obligations incurred as a result of GATT.

The WTO Safeguards Agreement defines serious injury as a significant overall impairment in the position of a domestic industry. In determining whether serious injury is present, investigating authorities are to evaluate all relevant factors having a bearing on the condition of the industry. Threat of serious injury is a threat that is clearly imminent as shown by facts, and not based on mere allegation, conjecture or remote possibility. If present serious injury is not found, a safeguard measure nevertheless can be applied if a threat of serious injury is found.

A domestic industry is defined as the producers as a whole of the like or directly competitive products operating within the territory of a Member, or producers who collectively account for a major proportion of the total domestic production of those products. A determination of serious injury cannot be made unless there is objective evidence of the existence of a causal link between increased imports of the product concerned and serious injury.

- Safeguard measures in RTAs

With respect to safeguard measures, a number of RTAs have gone beyond the WTO framework either by eliminating the possibility of using these measures, or by strengthening WTO rules to minimise the opportunity to use them in a protectionist manner.[20)]

Safeguard regulations in RTAs are usually divided in rules regarding the application of bilateral or regional safeguard measures and those that regulate the application of global safeguard actions. Basically, many RTAs simply confirm the global safeguard rules provided in the WTO rules and extensively regulate their bilateral or regional safeguard rules.[21)]

Bilateral safeguard measures are applied by one country against a product of another country when said product is imported in such increased quantities and under such conditions as to cause injury to the competing local industry.[22)] Since they are applicable only between the Parties to an RTA, their construction is flexible and may be adjusted to the very particular needs of the RTA Parties.

Regional safeguard measures are applied only to imports destined to a specific region within the importing country, or applied to exports of a product coming only from a certain region of the exporting country.[23] Because regional safeguards are not normally regulated under the WTO rules, there is flexibility in the construction of regional safeguard rules.

Global safeguard measures apply to a product, regardless of its origin, when the imported product causes injury to the competing domestic industry.[24] RTAs usually adopt GATT Article XIX and the WTO Agreement on Safeguards. RTAs that regulate global safeguards concentrate on the exceptions to the relevant WTO regulations. The most common exceptions are those regarding compensation or retaliation and exclusion from the action.

Bilateral safeguards in some RTA are also applicable only during a transitional period. Transitional safeguard actions were designed to allow the Parties to adjust and protect themselves against unexpected surges in trade after the RTA takes effect which may cause damage to some of their individual domestic industries. After the transitional period, the application of bilateral measures becomes more difficult for the Parties and only the global measures as generally set forth in the WTO Agreements subsist.

Many RTAs rules the compensation and the timing for compensation. Most RTAs allow the exporting party to apply compensation or practice specific retaliations immediately after the safeguard measure is applied by the importing Party. That is not the case with the WTO rules which allows the importing party to be free from any action by the exporting country for three years after the application of the measure. Some RTA provisions rule their own consultation procedures. They provide their parties with opportunities to find other ways to remedy the situation. On the other hand, dispute settlement procedure is not a common part of safeguard regulations of many RTAs because the RTAs usually contemplate dispute settlement procedures separately.

- Possible safeguard rules in the CJK FTA[25)]

Regarding trade remedy measures, there may be two approaches to construction of the provisions of the CJK FTA. Firstly, it is worth comparing the provisions of the already established RTAs in this region. In this method, several options on certain issues for the CJK FTA can be found comparing the provisions of the RTAs together with the WTO rules on trade remedies. Secondly, it is needed to consider the policies of the three countries on trade remedies and RTAs. The relationships among the countries on trade remedies are also required to consider in this procedure.

With respect to safeguard measures among trade remedies, many RTAs have gone beyond the WTO framework, either by eliminating the possibility of using these measures, or by strengthening WTO rules to minimise the opportunity of using them in a protectionist manner.

Safeguard regulations in RTAs are usually divided in rules

regarding the application of bilateral safeguard measures and those that regulate the application of global safeguard actions. Basically, many RTAs simply confirm the global safeguard rules provided in the WTO rules and extensively regulate their bilateral safeguard rules. This is because the parties of RTAs must consider the relationships with the third countries on global safeguards. However, they may feel that it is easier to produce articles on bilateral safeguards in their RTAs. Therefore, bilateral safeguards can be regulated in more detailed articles of the CJK FTA. Global safeguard measures may also be allowed in the FTA, just reaffirming the WTO rules. However, it will be difficult to imagine producing the special treatment rule for small/developing economy countries.

Regarding the issue of requirements for safeguards, the CJK FTA may allow that it does not require unforeseen development to take the action. Many RTAs in the Northeast Asian region are in this position and the three countries will prefer protecting their domestic industry. In contrast, the CJK FTA must require that imports should be a substantial cause of injury for the safeguard action. It is because the Parties will require a more substantial concept linking imports and injury to avoid disputes among the Parties. Conclusively, the standard of requirement for safeguard measures in the CJK FTA can be such that the imports substantially cause serious injury (or disturbances) or threat thereof to the domestic industry producing a like or directly competitive product.

The forms of safeguard measures in the CJK FTA may include suspension of the further reduction of customs duty under the FTA schedule. Furthermore, it may allow for the rate of customs duty to be increased with specific limitations such as the WTO MFN principle. The duration of the safeguard measure in the CJK FTA must be as long as necessary to prevent or remedy injury with specific period limitations. One year or two years with the same possible period of extension can be considered to be those specific period limitations.

The CJK FTA will provide the consultation and the compensation processes. Many RTAs have rules on the compensation issues. Most RTAs allow the exporting party to apply compensation or practise specific retaliation immediately after the safeguard measure is applied by the importing Party. That is not the case with the WTO rules which allow the importing party to be free from any action by the exporting country for three years after the application of the measure. RTAs also normally regulate their own consultation procedures. They provide their Parties with opportunities to find other ways to remedy the situation.

Regarding the consultation and compensation procedure, the CJK FTA shall permit various methods. Basically, the importing country proposing to apply a safeguard measure must provide trade liberalising compensation in other areas with the agreement of the exporting country as a first step. If they cannot reach agreement, the exporting country of the CJK FTA must have the right to suspend other concessions by retaliation.

Finally, the CJK FTA may also consider providing articles preventing the Party from exercising any of these two steps for a specific period.

3. What can we do for the domestic laws of the Member states?

RTA relationships may make the changes of domestic laws of a member country. As an example, there are several regulations that have provisions concerning RTAs or FTAs in Korea. Among them, Customs law and Law on the Inspection of Unfair Trade Act and Trade Remedies[26)] are major substantive laws. These laws provide several special articles regarding FTAs. For example, Article 22-3,[27)] 22-4,[28)] 22-5[29)] and 22-6[30)] of the Inspection of Unfair Trade Act and Trade Remedies are special provisions in relation to FTAs. There are also special laws regarding FTAs such as 'Act on Special Cases of the Customs Act for the Implementation of Free Trade Agreements.'

There are discussions on legislating for a general law covering processes of RTAs negotiations and the execution of RTAs. For example, there are some opinions that the Korean National Assembly must have active involvement in the decision-making process regarding the trade policies. According to the opinions, many major difficulties in the decision-making process and for the implementation of FTAs can be resolved emphasising the active role of the Assembly and the cooperation or share in responsibilities between the legislative and the administrative authorities.[31)]

Many other Korean laws are related to the issue of RTAs or FTAs direct and indirect ways. For example, there are several laws regarding the re-organisation of domestic industries with the FTA policy such as 'Special Act on Assistance to Farmers, Fishermen, etc. following the Conclusion of Free Trade Agreements' and 'Act on Trade Adjustment Assistance Following the Free Trade Agreements'.

In the point of the domestic laws, some of Northeast Asian countries still need more legal reforms to comply with international or Asian standards. Therefore, the legal cooperation among the members is also needed in this dimension. Korea's experience of economic and political development from its developing stage to now can be helpful. The cooperation in this sector also requires intense the exchange of human resources.

However, it is important to note that the legal cooperation should be done step by step to maximise the chance of success. With respect to the legal system of Korea, trade regulations and standards set by RTAs are considered a kind of economic resources - namely "Legal Infrastructure" - because a country that has various and sound trade regulations set by RTAs will benefit by the increase in trade resulted from these RTAs, meaning that this country is equipped with many legal infrastructures promoting a sound economic growth.

IV. Concluding Remarks

The concept of RTA is an important exception to the MFN principle in the WTO system. RTAs and WTO agreements make up the dual resources in the field of International Economic/Trade Law. These two rules are closely related with each other. Several articles in the WTO legal system such as Article XXIV of GATT have an important role in their rink to RTAs. Furthermore, the WTO has made various efforts to regulate RTAs in its framework. However, the issues regarding the relationships of RTAs and the WTO rules still encompass many problems.

The Northeast Asian region had not been active in the phenomenon of RTAs until the 1990s. However, the countries in this region changed this attitude after the Uruguay Round. Sometimes they even became parties to the WTO dispute cases on RTAs. The three countries in the region already have many RTAs and they are continuing to negotiate a range of RTAs. Therefore, a number of similarities and differences among the approaches of the countries to RTAs can be identified comparing their RTAs.

The CJK FTA is not just a dream for someone. The three countries started to consider the construction of this formal trade and economic cooperation tool. If they negotiate for the FTA, there must be a lot of points to remember. Legal aspect which is one of the main points related to the FTA needs more various researches and studies. For example, the safeguard issue is important for reducing the disputes between the parties of the RTA. The designers of the CJK FTA provisions must fully understand the policies of each party and the results of the FTA negotiations. Most of all, they will consider the relationship between RTAs and WTO system.

The CJK FTA will be unavoidable causes to change some parts of domestic laws of the members. In general, future domestic legislations and amendments in the members need to be done with the direction of complying with the principles of promoting cooperation, investment or exchanges rather than fine restrictions. Furthermore, the member countries must take many opportunities to share their opinions for the harmonised domestic laws. This movement will be helpful to business entities and human resources of members seeking chances in the CJK FTA era, and helpful to ensure the future growth engine by increasing trade relationship in the region.

1) See more, Elena Ianchovichina and Terrie Walmsley, "The impact of China's WTO Accession on East Asia", World Bank Policy Research Working Paper, World Bank, August 2003.

2) Zhang Jianping, *Analysis on the Issues of and Prospects for a China-Korea FTA*, Korea Institute for International Economic Policy, Seoul, 2006, p. 12.

3) Bongchul Kim, *Understanding Free Trade Agreement*, Intel Education Publishing, Seoul, 2004, p. 183.

4) Juliana W. Chen, "Achieving Supreme Excellence: How China is using Agreements with ASEAN to Overcome Obstacles to its leadership in Asian Regional Economic Integration", Chicago Journal of International Law (Vol. 7), University of Chicago Law School, 2007, pp. 660-662.

5) Kim, Dong-Hoon and Kim, Bong-Chul, "The Regional Trade Agreements of China, Korea and Japan", HUFS Law Review (Vol. 28), Hankuk University of Foreign Studies, November 2007, pp. 431-432.

6) Japan normally uses Economic Partnership Agreement (EPA) as the name of their RTAs. [Ministry of Economy, Trade and Industry, "Japan' s Policy on FTAs/EPAs", March 2005, p. 1.]

7) The political influence of the agricultural sector is still high in Japan and farmers have been a major obstacle in the Japanese trade liberalisation drive.

8) Jeong-Pyo Hong, *Regional Integration in Northeast Asia: Approaches to Integration Among China, Korea and Japan*, Korea Institute for International Economic Policy, Seoul, 2004, p. 13.

9) See more, Chang Jae Lee et al., *Rationale for a China-Japan-Korea FTA and Its Impact on the Korean Economy*, Korea Institute for International Economic Policy, Seoul, 2005.

10) See more, Wen Hai and Xi Zhang, "A Bilateral or Trilateral FTA?", in Yoon Hyung Kim and Chang Jae Lee (Eds.), *Strengthening Economic*

Cooperation in Northeast Asia, Korea Institute for International Economic Policy, Seoul, 2004, pp. 137-162.

11) See more, Fukunari Kimura, "Toward Formal Economic Integration in Northeast Asia: Beginning with a Bilateral FTA" in Yoon Hyung Kim and Chang Jae Lee (Eds.), *Ibid.*, pp. 115-136.

12) The ASEAN+3 RTA idea has enough and positive possibility. However, there are still many questions to make answer and barriers to overcome.

13) See more, Trilateral Joint Research of China, Korea and Japan, *Joint Report and Policy Recommendations concerning A Free Trade Agreement among China, Korea and Japan*, Development Research Center(China)/National Institute for Research Advancement(Japan)/ Korea Institute for International Economic Policy(Korea), 11 December 2006.

14) Fukunari Kimura and Mitsuyo Ando, "Obstacles and Variables of Northeast Asian FTA(s): Economic Obstacles", The KIEP-NAEAK International Conference Prospects for Regional FTA(s) in Northeast Asia, December 2006, p. 11.

15) Sung-Hoon Park, "Regionalism, Open Regionalism and Article XXIV GATT: Conflict and Harmony" in Francis Snyder (Ed.), *Regional and Global Regulation of International Trade*, Hart Publishing, Oxford, 2002, p. 275.

16) Bongchul Kim, *FTA-The Legal Points*, Korea Corporate Legal Affairs Association, Seoul, 2007, pp. 26-30.

17) In fact, paragraph 3 of the Enabling Clause merely requires that "any differential and more favourable treatment provided under this clause shall be designed to facilitate and promote the trade of developing countries and not to raise barriers to or create undue difficulties for the trade of any other Member."

18) See more, Bong-Chul Kim, *Lectures on FTAs and RTAs*, Korean Studies Information, 2009, pp. 67-80.

19) Although they are not enough many, some cases in the WTO dispute settlement mechanism about this issue.

20) Bong-Chul Kim, "Trade Remedy Rules in Regional Trade Agreements", Trade Remedy Review (Vol. 22), Korean Ministry of Commerce, Industry and Energy, April 2006, p. 156.

21) See more, Robert Teh, Thomas J. Prusa and Michele Budetta, "Trade Remedy Provisions in Regional Trade Agreements", Staff working paper, WTO, September 2007.

22) Generally, the rules for bilateral safeguards are often set out as extra provisions.

23) Under a regional safeguard, a party to a multilateral RTA can apply a safeguard measure against all or some of the members of that RTA or it can apply a safeguard for a certain region within its territory.

24) Global safeguards under WTO rules do not distinguish between exporting Parties.

25) See more, Dong-Hoon Kim and Bong-Chul Kim, "Safeguard measures in RTAs and proposals for the KCJ FTA", International Area Review (Vol. 11, No. 1), Hankuk University of Foreign Studies, May 2008, pp. 53-94.

26) Act on the Investigation of Unfair International Trade Practices and Remedy against Injury to Industry.

27) Safeguard Measures by Free Trade Agreements with Foreign States.

28) Abatement of Implementation of Safeguard Measures against FTA

29) Trade Damage Support Measures on Increase in Import of Special Goods following FTA.

30) Cooperation with Foreign State after FTA.

31) Park Chang-Hyun, *The Role of the National Assembly in the Process of Trade Negotiation*, Korea Legislation Research Institute, 2008, pp. 177-178.

This Chapter is based on author's presentation paper in the East Asian Regional Development International Conference (December 6. 2012) titled *The Korean FTAs and the Implication for the Northeast Asian Trade.*

Chapter 2.
Proposals for the threshold volume and margin for the application of trade remedy measures of an East Asia FTA

I. Introduction

II. Safeguard measure

III. Anti-dumping and Subsidy and Countervailing measures

IV. Concluding remarks

Proposals for the threshold volume and margin for the application of trade remedy measures of an East Asia FTA

Bongchul Kim and Ho Kim

I. Introduction

As we have seen after the formation of the WTO, Preferential Trade Agreements (PTAs) proliferate recently. According to a WTO statistic, 488 PTAs of the 612 PTAs have been notified to the WTO after 1995.[1] In spite of the fact that the WTO uses the term "RTAs" in its organizational body and in its documents, the term "PTAs" is more adequate than the term "RTAs" since the WTO member countries are growingly concluding trade agreements with their trading partners located at a long distance from them compared with those in the past among the neighboring countries.[2)]

Many PTAs have also been concluded between countries in East Asia. As regional integration has deepened with many bilateral FTAs in the region, a movement for an economic integration at the region-wide level arises. There are 5 ASEAN+1 FTAs (with Australia/New Zealand, China, India, Japan, and Korea). China, Japan, and Korea are negotiating a China-Japan-Korea trilateral FTA. The ASEAN and its "dialogue partners", namely, Australia, China, India, Japan, Korea, and New Zealand are now negotiating the Regional Comprehensive Economic Partnership (RCEP, also known as ASEAN+6).

This chapter presents some proposals for the provisions regarding the threshold volume and margin for the application of safeguard measures, anti-dumping and countervailing duty measures of a possible East Asia FTA. It also considers the possibility of providing preferential treatment for developing country members of an East Asia FTA. For this purpose, relevant provisions of selected PTAs as shown in the table below concluded between countries in East Asia were examined.

This chapter assumes a possible East Asia FTA in which at least China, Japan, Korea and the ASEAN will participate. It is also worth noting that this paper assumes that an East Asia FTA will have both types of safeguards, in other words, bilateral safeguards and global safeguards, considering the fact that the existing 5 ASEAN+1 FTAs all have both types of safeguards.

< Selected PTAs Examined>

Name	Name	Name	Name	Name
Korea-ASEAN Trade in Goods Agreement[3)]	ASEAN-China Trade in Goods Agreement[4)]	Japan-ASE-AN CEPA[5)]	ASEAN-India Trade in Goods Agreement[6)]	ASEAN-Australia-New Zealand FTA[7)]
Korea-Singa-pore FTA[8)]	Korea-India CEPA[9)]	Korea-Aus-tralia FTA[10)]	China-New Zealand FTA[11)]	China-Singa-pore FTA[12)]
Japan-Singa-pore EPA[13)]	Japan-India CEPA[14)]	New Zea-land-Malaysia FTA[15)]	New Zea-land-Singa-pore CEPA[16)]	Singapore-Australia FTA[17)]
India-Singa-pore CECA[18)]	Australia-New Zealand CERTA[19)]	Australia-New Zealand Protocol[20)]	Australia-Thailand FTA[21)]	

II. Safeguard measure

According to Article 9.1 of the Safeguard Agreement,[22] a global safeguard measure shall not be applied to a developing country whose import share a product concerned in the importing country does not exceed 3% if the share of imports collectively does not account for more than 9% of total imports. In addition, according to Article 9.2 of the Safeguard Agreement, a developing country can apply a safeguard measure for the maximum period of up to 10 years, which is a 2 year-extension of the period allowed to the other non-developing counties. The provision also allows an advantage to a developing country with respect to the reapplication of a global safeguard measure to the product which has been subject to a measure.

1. Threshold volume for the application of a bilateral safeguard measure

Some of the PTAs examined provide that a bilateral safeguard measure cannot be applied to a *developing* country member of the PTA if import share of such a country individually does not exceed 3% of total imports of the good concerned from *the other PTA parties*, provided that those countries with less than 3% import share collectively account for not more than 9% of total imports of the good concerned from the other PTA parties.[23) These PTAs follow the attitude of Article 9.1 of the Safeguard Agreement except that the threshold is calculated based on the imports of the good concerned from the other PTA parties.

Some PTAs provide that a bilateral safeguard measure cannot be applied against a good originating in the territory of a PTA party, so long as its share of imports of the good concerned in the importing PTA party does not exceed 3% of the total imports from *the PTA parties.*[24) China-Singapore provides that a bilateral safeguard measure cannot be applied against a good originating in the territory of a PTA party, so long as its share of imports of the good concerned in the importing PTA party does not exceed 3% of the *total imports of the good concerned in the importing PTA party.*[25) India-Singapore provides that a bilateral safeguard measure cannot be applied against a good originating in the territory of a PTA party if imports of the good concerned represent less than 2% of *market share* in terms of domestic sales *or* less than 3% of *total imports*.[26)] The rest of the PTAs examined do not have provisions regarding de *minimis* volume for the exemption from a safeguard measure and preferences for a developing country member of the PTAs.

Firstly, considering a need of internal trade liberalization through PTAs and a need of providing a preference to a developing country member of an East Asia FTA as an incentive for such countries' participating in an East Asia FTA, it is desirable for an East Asia FTA to set a higher level of *de minimis* volume applicable only to developing member countries, in addition to one which will be applied to all the other PTA member states. If that is the case, a need to maintain a collective share standard will be low as long as such collective share is not high enough to constitute a (substantial) cause of serious injury.

Secondly, even if an East Asia FTA set a *de minimis* volume, a question of whether the threshold volume should be calculated based on imports from *all countries* or whether it should be based on imports from *only the parties to an East Asia FTA* must be answered. As shown above, the PTAs examined are divided in this respect. Considering the fact that a safeguard measure is needed to remedy serious injury which occurs to domestic industry, it is better to calculate the threshold volume based on imports from *all countries* than it being calculated based on imports from only the parties to an East Asia FTA. Thus, a threshold such as "2% import share" for each member state of an East Asia FTA and "4% import share" for each developing country member of an East Asia FTA may be set.

Although the proposal above is a possible solution for an East Asia FTA, there is one remaining question to be considered with respect to the calculation of the threshold volume. That is whether the threshold volume should be calculated based on "*import* share" or "*market* share". An opinion argues that, regarding the calculation of negligible volume in anti-dumping or countervailing duty measures, a market share test is more sensible than an import share test.[27)] Considering the common nature of anti-dumping, countervailing duty, and safeguard measures as trade remedies to deal with injury to domestic industry, this opinion can be extended to the case of safeguard measures.

In fact, among the PTAs examined, India-Singapore adopts a combination of a market share test and an import share test in calculating threshold volume.[28)] The PTA lowers the possibility of the application of a bilateral safeguard measure by introducing a market share standard. For example, according to the PTA, a bilateral safeguard measure cannot be applied against imports from the other PTA party if market share of that party is less than 2% though its import share is more than 3% of total imports. This kind of combination method may be useful in a country-to-country basis PTA.

However, it will not be a desirable option for an East Asia FTA which will consist of many developing countries and other countries since different standards may be used depending on the circumstances of each exporting country. Therefore, the proposal presented here is that an East Asia FTA will adopt a *de minimis* volume of 1% *market* share for a party to an East Asia FTA and 2% *market* share for a developing country member of an East Asia FTA. If an East Asia FTA consists of ASEAN+6 or fewer number of countries, even collective share of *de minimis* volume will not be high enough to constitute a (substantial) cause of serious injury. In addition, this volume standard may be applied also to review cases for extension of a measure.

Regarding the question of whether to provide a developing country member of an East Asia FTA with some preferences which are similar to those set out in Article 9.2 of the Safeguard Agreement for a case where it applies a global safeguard measure - that is a 2 year-extension of the period allowed to the other non-developing counties -, a need to provide such preferences is not high if an East Asia FTA sets a short transition period and a short duration of a bilateral safeguard measure.

2. Threshold volume for the application of a global safeguard measure

No PTAs examined have special provisions regarding *de minimis* volume and special treatment for developing countries. Thus, all these PTAs follow the requirements of the Safeguard Agreement.

Considering a need of internal trade liberalization by exempting the PTA parties from safeguard measures and a need of balancing bilateral safeguards and global safeguards, the proposal presented in the previous section can be extended to the application of a global safeguard measure to the parties to an East Asia FTA. Thus, an East Asia FTA may adopt a *de minimis* volume of 1% market share for a party to an East Asia FTA and 2% market share for a developing country member of an East Asia FTA. In addition, this volume standard may be applied also to a mid-term review and an extension of a measure.

Regarding the question of whether to provide a developing country member of an East Asia FTA with some preferences in case where it applies a global safeguard measure to the other parties, a need to provide the preferences set out in Article 9.2 of the Safeguard Agreement still remains if an East Asia FTA does not set a short duration of a global safeguard measure.

III. Anti-dumping and Subsidy and Countervailing measures

Article 5.8 of the Anti-dumping Agreement[29] and Article 11.9 of the SCM Agreement[30] provide that an application for the initiation of an anti-dumping or a countervailing duty investigation shall be rejected and an investigation shall be terminated promptly if the margin of dumping or subsidy is *de minimis*, or if the volume of dumped or subsidized imports, or the injury is negligible. For anti-dumping cases, Article 5.8 of the Anti-dumping Agreement provides that the *de minimis* dumping margin is less than 2% of the export price and that the negligible volume of dumped imports is less than 3% of total imports if countries whose import share individually account for less than 3% collectively account for not more than 7% of total imports. For countervailing duty cases, Article 11.9 of the SCM Agreement provides that the *de minimis* subsidy margin is less than 1% *ad valorem*, but the Article does not set a standard for the negligible volume of subsidized imports. For developing countries, Article 27.10 of the SCM Agreement presents 2% of its value, and individual import share of 4% subject to collective import share of 9%, respectively. Article 18.3 of the Anti-dumping Agreement and Article 32.3 of the SCM Agreement provide that all provisions of those agreements shall apply to investigations and reviews.

1. Threshold dumping or subsidy margin

Among the PTAs examined, only New Zealand-Singapore has special provisions regarding this matter. Article 9.1(a) of New Zealand-Singapore provides that the *de minimis* dumping margin is increased from 2% of the export price to 5%. Article 9.1(b) of New Zealand-Singapore extends this new standard to review cases by providing that the new de minimis margin is applied not only in new cases but also in refund and review cases. Regarding the negligible volume, Article 9.1(c) of New Zealand-Singapore provides that the negligible volume of 3% of imports is raised to 5% in anti-dumping cases. However, Article 9.1(c) of New Zealand-Singapore maintains the 7% collective import share by providing that existing cumulation provisions under Article 5.8 of the Anti-dumping Agreement continue to apply. Thus, a party to New Zealand-Singapore can be exempt from an anti-dumping measure taken by the other PTA party if its import share is less than 5% and the collective import share of the party and non-PTA countries whose import share is less than 3%

does not account for more than 7% of total imports. The rest of the PTAs examined do not have any special provisions regarding this matter. Thus, these PTAs follow the provisions of the WTO disciplines.

Regarding the *de minimis* dumping or subsidy margin, as shown above, only New Zealand-Singapore has a reinforced standard of 5% of the export price. However, this standard is applied only to anti-dumping cases. There is no PTA examined which has a reinforced standard for subsidy margin. With respect to this matter, an opinion argues that the level of *de minimis* margin of dumping and subsidy should be raised and this reinforced standard should be applied to both investigation and review cases.[31)] Considering a need of internal trade liberalization by limiting the application of trade remedies to the PTA partners and considering the common nature of anti-dumping and countervailing duty measures, it is desirable for an East Asia FTA to adopt such a reinforced standard for *de minimis* dumping and subsidy margin.

Regarding the negligible volume for an exemption from anti-dumping and countervailing duty measures, as shown above, only New Zealand-Singapore has a reinforced standard of 5% of total imports in anti-dumping cases. However, the PTA still maintains the 7% collective import share. There is no PTAs examined which has a reinforced negligible volume standard for countervailing duty measures. As shown above, an opinion argues that, regarding the calculation of negligible volume in anti-dumping or countervailing duty measures, a market share test is more sensible than an import share test.[32] In fact, an EU regulation applies a "1% market share subject to 3% collective market share" test in anti-dumping cases.[33]

Considering the common nature of anti-dumping and countervailing duty measures as trade remedies to deal with injury to domestic industry, an East Asia FTA may adopt a market share test in both anti-dumping and countervailing duty cases. And as explained in Section 3, when a threshold which will be applied to all PTA parties is set, a need to maintain a collective share standard will be low as long as such collective share is not high enough to constitute a cause of material injury.

At this point, an important difference between anti-dumping measures and countervailing duty measures should be considered. With respect to *de minimis* margin and negligible volume, the Anti-dumping Agreement does not provide any preferences with developing countries as in Article 27.10 of the SCM Agreement. This is probably because dumping is considered as an unfair practice of individual producers, compared to subsidies which are recognized by Article 27.1 of the SCM Agreement as an important instrument in economic development of developing countries. Thus, if an East Asia FTA adopts this concept, it may not provide such preferences in anti-dumping cases.

2. Threshold dumping or subsidy negligible volume

There is one more question which should be answered with respect to the matter of negligible volume for countervailing duty measures. As shown above, the SCM Agreement does not set a standard for the negligible volume of subsidized imports except the one for developing countries provided for in Article 27.10 of the agreement. In light of a need to set a clear standard, an East Asia FTA may set a negligible volume standard applicable to the non-developing country member states which is lower than the one for the developing country member states. It is noticeable that an EU regulation applies a "1% market share subject to 3% collective market share" test in countervailing duty cases,[34)] while it applies to developing countries the same standard as Article 27.10 of the SCM Agreement which is an "individual import share of 4% subject to collective import share of 9%."[35)]

Therefore, the proposal presented here is that an East Asia FTA may adopt a reinforced standard for *de minimis* margin of dumping and negligible volume which is applicable to all parties to an East Asia FTA, for example, a *de minimis* dumping margin of 5% of the export price and a volume of 2% market share. For countervailing duty measures, an East Asia FTA may adopt, for example, a *de minimis* margin of 3% *ad valorem* and a volume of 1% market share, and a *de minimis* margin of 5% *ad valorem* and a volume of 2% market share for developing country members of an East Asia FTA.

A related question arises with respect to whether the de miminis margin and negligible volume may also be applied to review cases. As shown above, Article 18.3 of the Anti-dumping Agreement and Article 32.3 of the SCM Agreement provide that all provisions of those agreements shall apply to investigations and reviews. Among the PTAs examined, New Zealand-Singapore extends its reinforced *de minimis* dumping margin to review cases.[36] Thus, under this PTA, an anti-dumping measure subject to an interim review, a sunset review, or a new comer review shall be terminated if the margin of dumping is less than *de minimis*. However, this PTA does not provide an extension of the negligible volume standard to review cases. This PTA does not extend the *de minimis* margin of subsidy and negligible volume set out in Article 11.9 and Article 27.10 of the SCM Agreement to review cases, either. The rest of the PTAs examined do not have any special provisions regarding this matter.

Although a WTO panel concluded that the *de minimis* standard for an investigation set out in Article 5.8 of the Anti-dumping Agreement does not apply to sunset reviews under Article 11.3 of the Anti-dumping Agreement,[37] such an explanation appears not to be highly convincing considering the existence of Article 18.3 of the Anti-dumping Agreement and Article 32.3 of the SCM Agreement.

And considering the similarities between an investigation and a review, an East Asia FTA may provide that the *de minimis* dumping or subsidy margin set out in an East Asia FTA shall be applied to review cases.[38] And if that is the case, it is also possible for an East Asia FTA to extend the negligible volume of dumped or subsidized imports set out in an East Asia FTA to review cases. However, the negligible volume of dumped or subsidized imports set out in an East Asia FTA will not be applied to reviews for refund cases under Article 9.3 of the Anti-dumping Agreement, reviews for exporters not investigated under Article 9.4 of the Anti-dumping Agreement and Article 19.3 of the SCM Agreement, and new comer reviews under Article 9.5 of the Anti-dumping Agreement, since those reviews concern an individual margin of dumping or subsidy of a producer or exporter.

To these reviews, the *de minimis* dumping or subsidy margin will be applied. The proposal presented here will be meaningful if an East Asia FTA sets a time restriction on the reapplication of an anti-dumping or countervailing duty measure against the products imported from the PTA parties. This is because a measure may be extended if the required conditions are met, while such a measure shall be terminated if the required conditions are not met and certain period of time must elapse before the reapplication of a new measure.

IV. Concluding remarks

This chapter presents a proposal for safeguards of setting a de minimis volume of 1% market share for a party to an East Asia FTA and 2% market share for a developing country member of an East Asia FTA, based on examining relevant provisions of selected PTAs concluded between countries in East Asia. This proposal may be applied to the application of both bilateral and global safeguard measures, and this volume standard may be applied also to a mid-term review and review cases for extension of a measure.

For anti-dumping measures, the proposal is that an East Asia FTA may adopt a reinforced standard for de minimis margin of dumping and negligible volume which is applicable to all parties to an East Asia FTA, for example, a de minimis dumping margin of 5% of the export price and a volume of 2% market share. For countervailing duty measures, an East Asia FTA may adopt, for example, a de minimis margin of 3% *ad valorem* and a volume of 1% market share, and a de minimis margin of 5% *ad valorem* and a volume of 2% market share for developing country members of an East Asia FTA. And the de miminis margin and negligible volume may also be applied to review cases.

The authors hope that the proposals for an East Asia FTA may also give an indication to future PTAs and multilateral trade negotiations.

1) *Regional Trade Agreements: Facts and Figures*, WORLD TRADE ORGANIZATION, http://www.wto.org/english/tratop_e/region_e/regfac_e.htm (last visited June 5, 2015).

2) Thomas Cottier & Marina Foltea, *Constitutional Functions of the WTO and Regional Trade Agreements*, *in* REGIONAL TRADE AGREEMENTS AND THE WTO LEGAL SYSTEM 43, 44 n.2 (Lorand Bartels & Federico Ortino eds., 2006).

3) Agreement on Trade in Goods Under the Framework Agreement on Comprehensive Economic Cooperation Among the Governments of the Republic of Korea and the Member Countries of the Association of Southeast Asian Nations, Aug. 24, 2006, *available at* http://www.fta.go.kr/main/situation/kfta/lov5/asean/2/ [hereinafter Korea-ASEAN Trade in Goods].

4) Agreement on Trade in Goods of the Framework Agreement on Comprehensive Economic Cooperation Between the Association of Southeast Asian Nations and the People's Republic of China, Nov. 29, 2004, *available at* http://www.asean.org/communities/asean-economic-community/category/free-trade-agreements-with-dialogue-partners [hereinafter ASEAN-China Trade in Goods].

5) Agreement on Comprehensive Economic Partnership Among Japan and Member States of the Association of Southeast Asian Nations, Apr. 14, 2008, available at http://www.asean.org/communities/asean-economic-community/category/free-trade-agreements-with-dialogue-partners [hereinafter Japan-ASEAN].

6) Agreement on Trade in Goods Under the Framework Agreement on Comprehensive Economic Cooperation Between the Association of Southeast Asian Nations and the Republic of India, Aug. 13, 2009, available at http://www.asean.org/communities/asean-economic-community/category/free-trade-agreements-with-dialogue-partners [hereinafter ASEAN-India Trade in Goods].

7) Agreement Establishing the ASEAN-Australia-New Zealand Free Trade Area, Feb. 27, 2009, 2672 U.N.T.S. 3, available at https://

treaties.un.org/doc/Publication/UNTS/Volume%202672/v2672.pdf [hereinafter ASEAN-Australia-New Zealand].

8) Free Trade Agreement, S. Kor.-Sing., Aug. 4, 2005, *available at* http://www.fta.go.kr/main/situation/kfta/lov5/sg/.

9) Comprehensive Economic Partnership Agreement, India-S. Kor., Aug. 7, 2009, *available at* http://www.fta.go.kr/main/situation/kfta/lov5/in/.

10) Free Trade Agreement, Austl.-S. Kor., Apr. 8, 2014, *available at* http://www.fta.go.kr/main/situation/kfta/lov3/au/1/.

11) Free Trade Agreement, China-N.Z., Apr. 7, 2008, 2590 U.N.T.S. 101, *available at* https://treaties.un.org/doc/Publication/UNTS/Volume%20 2590/v2590.pdf.

12) Free Trade Agreement, China-Sing., Oct. 23, 2008, *available at* http://www.fta.gov.sg/fta_csfta.asp?hl=27 [hereinafter China-Singapore].

13) Agreement Between Japan and the Republic of Singapore for a New-Age Economic Partnership, Japan-Sing., Jan. 13, 2002, 2739 U.N.T.S. ----, *available at* http://www.mofa.go.jp/policy/economy/fta/index.html.

14) Comprehensive Economic Partnership Agreement, India-Japan, Feb. 16, 2011, 2862 U.N.T.S. ----, *available at* https://treaties.un.org/doc/Publication/UNTS/No%20Volume/50016/Part/I-50016-08000002803387cc.pdf.

15) Free Trade Agreement, Malay.-N.Z., Oct. 26, 2009, 2724 U.N.T.S. ----, *available at* https://treaties.un.org/doc/Publication/UNTS/No%20 Volume/48207/Part/I-48207-08000002802c6682.pdf .

16) Agreement Between New Zealand and Singapore on a Closer Economic Partnership, N.Z.-Sing., Nov. 14, 2000, 2203 U.N.T.S. 129, *available at* https://treaties.un.org/doc/Publication/UNTS/Volume%20 2203/v2203.pdf [hereinafter New Zealand-Singapore].

17) Free Trade Agreement, Austl.-Sing., Feb. 17, 2003, 2257 U.N.T.S. 103,

available at https://treaties.un.org/doc/Publication/UNTS/Volume%20 2257/v2257.pdf.

18) Comprehensive Economic Cooperation Agreement, India-Sing., June 29, 2005, *available at* http://www.fta.gov.sg/sg_fta.asp [hereinafter India-Singapore].

19) Closer Economic Relations Trade Agreement, Austl.-N.Z., Mar. 28, 1983, 1329 U.N.T.S. 175, *available at* https://treaties.un.org/doc/Publication/UNTS/Volume%201329/v1329.pdf.

20) Protocol to the Australia-New Zealand Closer Economic Relations Trade Agreement on Acceleration of Free Trade in Goods, Austl.-N.Z., Aug. 18, 1988, 1536 U.N.T.S. 71, *available at* https://treaties.un.org/doc/Publication/UNTS/Volume%201536/v1536.pdf.

21) Free Trade Agreement, Austl.-Thai., July 5, 2004, *available at* http://www.dfat.gov.au/fta/tafta/.

22) Agreement on Safeguards art. 9.1, Apr. 15, 1994, Marrakesh Agreement Establishing the World Trade Organization, Annex 1A, 1869 U.N.T.S. 154 [hereinafter Safeguard Agreement].

23) Japan-ASEAN, *supra* note 5, art. 20.3; ASEAN-Australia-New Zealand, *supra* note 7, ch. 7, art. 6.2.

24) Korea-ASEAN Trade in Goods, *supra* note 3, art. 9.7; ASEAN-China Trade in Goods, *supra* note 4, art. 9.7; ASEAN-India Trade in Goods, *supra* note 6, art. 10.7.

25) China-Singapore, *supra* note 12, art. 43.4.

26) India-Singapore, *supra* note 18, art. 2.9.2(f).

27) Aluisio de Lima-Campos, *Nineteen Proposals to Curb Abuse in Anti-dumping and Countervailing Duty Proceedings*, 39 J. WORLD TRADE 239, 247-49 (2005).

28) India-Singapore, *supra* note 18, art. 2.9.2(f).

29) Agreement on Implementation of Article VI of the General Agreement on Tariffs and Trade 1994 art. 5.8, Apr. 15, 1994, Marrakesh Agreement Establishing the World Trade Organization, Annex 1A, 1868 U.N.T.S. 201 [hereinafter Anti-dumping Agreement].

30) Agreement on Subsidies and Countervailing Measures art. 11.9, Apr. 15, 1994, Marrakesh Agreement Establishing the World Trade Organization, Annex 1A, 1869 U.N.T.S. 14 [hereinafter SCM Agreement].

31) Lima-Campos, *supra* note 27, at 258-60.

32) *Id.* at 247-49.

33) Council Regulation 1225/2009, of 30 November 2009 on Protection Against Dumped Imports from Countries Not Members of the European Community, art. 5.7, 2009 O.J. (L 343) 51, 60.

34) Council Regulation 597/2009, of 11 June 2009 on Protection Against Subsidised Imports from Countries Not Members of the European Community, art. 10.9, 2009 O.J. (L 188) 93, 101.

35) *Id.* art. 14.4.

36) New Zealand-Singapore, *supra* note 16, art. 9.1(b).

37) Panel Report, *United States — Sunset Review of Anti-Dumping Duties on Corrosion-Resistant Carbon Steel Flat Products from Japan*, ¶ 7.70, WT/DS244/R (Aug. 14, 2003).

38) See Lima-Campos, *supra* note 27, at 258-60 (arguing that Article 5.8 of the Anti-dumping Agreement and Article 11.9 of the SCM Agreement regarding the *de minimis* dumping or subsidy margin shall be applied to review cases).

This Chapter is based on author's presentation paper in the 2nd Joint International Conference on Korean Studies and Thai Studies (July 24-25. 2015) titled *Proposals for the threshold volume and margin for the application of trade remedy measures of an East Asia FTA.*

Chapter 3. Future implications in the Korea-EU FTA: The new meanings of the legal infrastructure

Future implications in the Korea-EU FTA: The new meanings of the legal infrastructure

Bongchul Kim and Ho Kim

I. Introduction

Much more than one-half of the international trade is performed under the preferential trade rules such as FTAs (Free Trade Agreements). The FTA style is the most popular legal tool in many preferential rules. The FTA networks are recently overlapping and the map is becoming more complicated with the proliferation of laws. Furthermore, some emerging issues on FTAs are related to the different legal aspects. Although many of the issues are still in the economic field, some FTA partners are now developing new meanings in their legal tools for other field.

Korea and the EU are important trading partners. They have been expanding cooperation in many areas. For the purpose, the Korea-EU FTA became the fundamental legal tool to provide more favourable environments regarding the Korea-EU economic relation since 2011. The Korea-EU FTA provides many types of preferential rules for the economic cooperation between the parties. The economic cooperation between the partners based on the FTA has been improved in many ways.

The two parties of the bilateral FTA are looking forward to developing new engines or fields for their benefits now. Here, there are several legal dimensions on the FTA to examine. The main purpose of this chapter is to discuss some legal issues on the Korea-EU FTA. The legal analysis on the FTA is directly related to the suggestion of new possible meanings of the agreement regarding other areas. The law can be an important new engine to boost more and better cooperation between the partners expanding the application of the law to other topics.

II. The Korea-EU FTA : The Legal Infrastructure for the Economic Cooperation

1. The Establishment of the FTA

With respect to the legal system of an FTA party, trade regulations and standards under FTAs are considered a kind of economic resources - namely 'Legal Infrastructure.' It is because a country that has various and sound trade regulations by FTAs will benefit with the trade increase resulted from these FTAs. That is to say, the country is equipped with many legal infrastructures promoting a sound economic growth.

When a WTO member enters into an FTA through which it grants more favourable conditions to its trade with other WTO member parties to that agreement than to other WTO members' trade, it basically departs from the non-discrimination principle defined in Article I of GATT and other rules. However, WTO Members can enter into such FTAs under specific conditions, which are spelled out in three sets of rules: *Article XXIV of the GATT; The so-called Enabling Clause; Article V of the GATS.*

The Korea-EU FTA is based on Article XXIV of the GATT and other related WTO rules. Therefore, the partners of the FTA and the WTO Members, Korea and EU, have justifiable exceptions to provide favourable trade conditions from the major principle of the multilateral WTO rules.

The Asian financial crisis was a momentum for the Korean FTA policy as one of the legal tools to propel economic benefit.[1] The government expected that FTAs can be the legal infrastructures for their recovery from the crisis with their systemic reforms. They intended to utilise FTAs in promoting qualitative growth of the economy and leap into a more advanced economy. For the purpose, Korea has established the FTA relations with many partners such as Chile, Singapore, EFTA, EU, ASEAN, India, Peru, Colombia, Turkey and the US. They recently finished the FTA negotiations with Canada and Australia, and are still underway with many other countries such as Mexico, Indonesia, Vietnam, New Zealand and China.

Korea is the EU's tenth largest trade partner, and the EU is Korea's fourth export destination (after China, Japan and the US) as well as the largest investors to Korea. They have various areas for their cooperation such as science and technology, education, statistics, maritime and fisheries, energy, environment, finance, customs and competition policy. To promote specific projects to expand cooperation, The Korea-EU Joint Committee Meeting at the deputy ministerial-level has been held annually since 2001.

After slowing down in 2009 due to the financial crisis, trade flows between them started to increase again in 2010. In 2011, Korea reached the important benchmark of $ 1 trillion total foreign trade (close to 100% of the Korean GDP). EU exports to Korea enjoyed an annual average growth rate of 7% between 2007 and 2011. As of 2012, the trade volume between Korea and the EU accounts for 9.3% of Korea's total trade volume based on the FTA system. The trade between the two FTA partners is dominated by power/non-electrical machinery, chemicals, transport equipment, optical and photo equipment and base metals. EU records a significant surplus in trade in services with Korea. EU provides to Korea specialised services in such sectors as banking, financial and accounting services and European companies are the largest investors in Korea.

The Korea-EU FTA became the fundamental legal infrastructure to provide more favourable environments regarding the Korea-EU economic relation. Negotiations on the FTA were launched in May 2007 in Seoul. After eight formal rounds of talks, the FTA was initialled by both sides on 15 October 2009. On 6 October 2010 the Agreement was officially signed during the EU-Korea Summit in Brussels. The Agreement has been provisionally applied since 1 July 2011.

2. The structure of the FTA provisions

The FTA comprises 15 Chapters, several annexes and appendixes, three protocols and four understandings. Chapter 1 explains the objectives and definitions of the parties throughout the agreement text. In sequence, Chapter 2 sets forth the objective of eliminating the barriers on trade in goods. Specific non-tariff barriers (NTBs) are also tackled in separated four annexes to the FTA (electronics, motor vehicles and parts, pharmaceutical products and medical devices, and chemicals of different types of standards).[2)]

Chapter 3 provides the use of trade remedies such as safeguards. Then, Chapter 4 intended to reduce obstacles as technical trade barriers. The main objective of Chapter 5 is to reduce the negative effects of Sanitary and Phytosanitary (SPS) Measures to facilitate trade between the partners while protecting human and animal or plant life. Chapter 6 aims to enhance cooperation in customs and trade facilitation matters. Chapter 7 covers liberalisation of trade in services and non-service sectors including telecommunications and transport. Chapter 8 is on the sector of the freely convertible currency and the chapter provides standard safeguards in this area. The partners of the FTA can use the measure for a period not exceeding 6 months in exceptional circumstances.

Chapter 9 contains provision to enhance access to government procurement. The FTA expands opportunities to public works concessions and 'Build-Operate-Transfer' (BOT) contracts.

Chapter 10 includes strong disciplines in important area as the intellectual property rights. Chapter 11 includes the competition regulations and a section on subsidies to prohibit certain types of subsidies. Chapter 12 provides strong transparency commitments in order to an efficient and predictable regulatory environment for economic operators, especially small ones doing business in their territories. It is significant that the FTA includes this provision because the lack of transparency of the regulatory environment has been a problem when European firms doing business in Korea.

Chapter 13 provides the regulations for the promotion of sustainable development in order to strengthen their trade relations and cooperation. It contains firm commitments to multilateral labour and environmental standards by both parties. Then, Chapter 14 has provisions on the effective and rapid dispute settlement as well a meditation mechanism for Non-Tariff Measures. Procedures of dispute settlement mechanism are on the basis of the WTO, but it's much faster here. Chapter 15 is about Institutional, General and Final provisions.

The FTA also includes three protocols. The first one is the protocol on Mutual Administrative Assistance in Custom Matter, the second one is the protocol on cultural cooperation, and the third one is the protocol on Croatian Accession. A protocol on cultural cooperation is to implement the protection and promotion of the diversity of cultural expressions in accordance with the UNESCO Convention.

Even if some FTA provisions on a certain area may satisfy the conditions of Article XXIV of the GATT, there are still other issues. Sometimes the issues come from the imperfection of the WTO rules in the area. This may be one of the reasons for some FTAs to provide more detailed or different rules than the WTO. Provisions on safeguard measures in FTAs can be an example for that.

<The Provisions of the Korea-EU FTA>

Chapter 1	Objectives and General Definitions
Chapter 2	National Treatment and Market Access For Goods
Chapter 3	Trade Remedies
Chapter 4	Technical Barriers to Trade
Chapter 5	Sanitary and Phytosanitary Measures
Chapter 6	Customs and Trade Facilitation
Chapter 7	Trade in Services, Establishment and Electronic Commerce
Chapter 8	Payments and Capital Movements
Chapter 9	Government Procurement
Chapter 10	Intellectual Property
Chapter 11	Competition
Chapter 12	Transparency
Chapter 13	Trade and Sustainable Development
Chapter 14	Dispute Settlement
Chapter 15	Institutional, General and Final Provisions
Protocols	Protocol Concerning the Definition of 'Origination Products' and Methods of Administrative Co-operation Protocol on Mutual Administrative Assistance in Custom Matters Protocol on Cultural Co-operation Protocol on Croatian Accession

3. Korean domestic laws on the FTA

With respect to the legal system of Korea, domestic trade regulations and standards under FTAs are considered a kind of legal Infrastructure. Therefore, FTA relationships may make the changes of domestic laws of a member country. As an example, there are several regulations that have provisions concerning FTAs in Korea. Among them, Customs law and Law on the Inspection of Unfair Trade Act and Trade Remedies[3] are major substantive laws. These laws provide several special articles regarding FTAs. For example, Article 22-3,[4] 22-4,[5] 22-5[6] and 22-6[7] of the Inspection of Unfair Trade Act and Trade Remedies are special provisions in relation to FTAs. There are also special laws regarding FTAs such as 'Act on Special Cases of the Customs Act for the Implementation of Free Trade Agreements.'

There are discussions on legislating for a general law covering processes of FTAs negotiations and the execution of their FTAs. For example, there are some domestic regulations that the Korean National Assembly must have active involvement in the decision-making process regarding the FTA trade policies. According to the rules, many major difficulties in the decision-making process and for the implementation of FTAs can be resolved emphasising the active role of the Assembly and the cooperation or share in responsibilities between the legislative and the administrative authorities.[8]

Many other Korean laws are related to the issue of FTAs in

direct and indirect ways. For example, there are several laws regarding the re-organisation of and the supports to domestic industries with the FTA policy such as 'Special Act on Assistance to Farmers, Fishermen, etc. following the Conclusion of Free Trade Agreements' and 'Act on Trade Adjustment Assistance Following the Free Trade Agreements'.

In the point of the domestic laws, Korea is still needed more legal changes to comply with international or FTA standards. Therefore, the legal cooperation among the members is also needed in this dimension. The cooperation in this sector also requires intense the exchange of human resources. However, it is important to note that the legal cooperation should be done step by step to maximise the chance of success.

III. The FTA on the North Korean issue

1. Special treatment to the 'Inter-Korean' transaction and the Gaesung Industrial Complex

The initial purpose of Korea's FTAs is mainly an economic one because its economy is largely dependent on trade with other countries. However, political reasons were added to the FTA policy. Regarding the North Korean issues, the government thought that the FTAs could be useful for the stability of the Korean Peninsula. Korea recognises the inter-Korean relationship as a special one and gives a preferential treatment to it according to the 'inter-Korean' transaction principle. They also expect for international society to recognise the 'inter-Korean' relationship as a basis for the preferential treatment. However, sometimes this unique treatment has possibility to conflict with the MFN principle of the WTO.[9)]

The idea of the Gaesung Industrial Complex (GIC) is based on the promotion of the inter-Korean economic cooperation. Although the project started for the economic benefits of the two Koreas, it is also a peace keeping project.[10] Then, Korean government has tried to make legal infrastructures for the GIC in their FTAs. Almost every Korean FTA has preferential provisions to recognise the products from the Complex in North Korea as (South) Korean based on the special and unique relationship between the two Koreas. Considering the GIC globalising policy of the Korean government, it is needed to see the special treatment provisions in the FTA.

The production of goods in the complex started in 2004. The inter-Korean agreement provided legal basis for the two governments to start the project. They also established the domestic legal frames to support the project in the territories of two parties. For example, the Gaesung Industrial District Management Committee (GIDMC or KIDMC), established by the Gaesung Industrial Zone Law in North Korea and authorized by the Act on the Support for the Gaesung Industrial District serves, administers, controls, and manages the Complex.[11] With the legal basis, companies can take various incentives from the governmental supports. 25 out of the 26 firms that began establishing operations in the area applied for the loans from the Inter-Korea Cooperation Fund in South Korea.[12]

The importance of the GIC business in the inter-Korean trade was 6% when it was started in 2004. However, it has increased steeply every year and eventually went beyond 50% in 2009. Even during the year 2010 with the sinking of the warship Cheonan and shelling of Yeonpyeong Island, the GIC was responsible for more than 76% or $1.4 billion out of the $1.9 billion in total inter-Korean trade after 2010.[13] The importance of GIC in inter-Korean trade, which is more than 99% since 2011, is absolute.

North Korea stopped all access to the area from the South, citing provocations from Seoul against its sovereign dignity and withdrew all 53,000 North Korean labourers in April 2013. It resulted in the suspension of operations at the joint industrial park.[14] The suspension of the project was one of a string of steps the North took in anger at annual joint US-South Korea military exercises, and the UN toughened its sanctions adopted after the North's third nuclear test in February 2013.[15]

The governments of the two Koreas were changed in 2013, and it is seems that both governments want to have the upper hand regarding the GIC. At the round of talks on the GIC normalisation, the South has repeatedly demanded the North provide a firm guarantee that it will not close the industrial area down in the future and set up a system to protect the safety and property of South Koreans who have invested and worked in the city.[16] South and North Korea have reached an agreement to normalise the operations at the GIC, 133 days after the complex was shut down. The agreement guaranteed that the complex would operate normally "without being affected by the political situation under any circumstances."

The South government softened on its demands that the North take full responsibility for the closure, while the North accepted a number of key demands, including internationalisation of the Complex. Actually, it has a policy to transform the Complex into an international manufacturing zone with the companies or funds from third countries. If companies of a third country came into the Complex, it would be hard for both governments to use the area as a political measure. South Korea calls for the North to guarantee the safety of its businessmen in the industrial park, and pressed the North to transform the complex into an international zone by adopting global standards of doing business.[17)]

The two Koreas have consented to guarantee business environments in the area that meet international standards, and work towards improving the competitiveness of Complex in the global market. The references to developing the area into a 'globally competitive' complex appeared to reflect the wishes of the South. The two Koreas will develop systems on labour, taxing, wages and insurance to meet international standards, and provide a lower trade barrier when trading to a third nation to improve the GIC's international competitiveness.[18)]

2. The special GIC provisions in the Korean FTAs

The Special Act on the Execution of the WTO Agreement in Korea was made to facilitate the application of Korean FTAs. Section 4 of Article 3 in the act declares the principles of 'inter-Korean' transaction and imposes obligations on the Korean government of making efforts for the internal transaction to be recognised in international society. Article 5 of the act also provides the 'inter-Korean' transaction principle. It can be a basis of the Korean domestic law for the preferential treatment.

There is no provision about the GIC in the Korea-Chile FTA because the GIC project was in its nascent stage at that time. Article 4.3 and 4.4 of the second Korean FTA, the Korea-Singapore FTA first provided special treatments of certain goods made at the Complex. Certain GIC-produced goods imported into Korea and exported to Singapore are treated as Korea-origin goods if the total value of non-originating inputs does not exceed 40% of the customs value of the final good for which originating status is claimed, the value of originating materials is not less than 45% of the customs value of the final good for which originating status is claimed, and the last process of production or operation takes place in Korea.

Article 13 and Appendix 4 to Annex I of the Korea-EFTA FTA provides a standard for the treatment of the GIC-produced goods as Korea-origin goods. The GIC-produced goods are considered as Korea-origin goods if the total value of non-originating input does not exceed 40% of the ex-works price of the final product for which originating status is claimed, and the value of originating materials exported from Korea is not less than 60% of the total value of materials used in manufacturing the re-imported material or product.

Annex 3 of the Korea-ASEAN FTA on trade in goods provides a standard for the treatment of the GIC-produced goods as Korea-origin goods. The standard is similar to that of the Korea-EFTA FTA, i.e., the ratio of non-originating input and originating materials from Korea is 4 to 6.[19)] Article 3.14 of the Korea-India CEPA, Annex 3-B and the notes exchanged by both parties also provide a standard for the GIC-produced goods as Korea-origin goods. The standard is similar to those of the Korea-EFTA FTA and the Korea-ASEAN FTA.

The Korea-US FTA does not directly permit special treatment of the GIC. It just provides a possibility of the treatment by establishing the 'Committee on Outward Processing Zones (OPZ) on the Korean Peninsula.' According to the Annex 22-B of the FTA, the Committee will discuss the criteria for OPZs like the GIC and the special treatment of the Zone under the FTA order. It was a concession of both parties because Korea considered the GIC as an important issue while the US worried about security problems from North Korea. It seems that the FTA system appears likely to have only a minimal impact on the US restrictions on North Korean imports and the controls of the North Korean issues.[20)]

Article 12 of the Protocol Concerning the Definition of Originating Products and Methods of Administrative Co-operation in the Korea-EU FTA provided the possibility for the special treatment of GIC as below;

> *3. Notwithstanding paragraphs 1 and 2 of this Article, the Parties agree that the certain goods shall be considered to be originating even if they have undergone working or processing outside of Korea, on materials exported from Korea and subsequently re-imported there, provided that the working or processing is done in the areas designed by Parties pursuant to Annex IV.*

Then, Annex IV of the protocol provides languages about the details on the concept of OPZs similar to those of the Korea-US FTA. It is because the Korea-EU FTA was concluded after the conclusion of the Korea-US FTA and the EU requested a similar level of concession compared with the Korea-US FTA.

3. Possibility of the improvement of the Human Rights in North Korea by the FTA?

The restriction on human rights in North Korea is accelerating. In North Korea where the state sovereignty and maintenance of system matter much, human rights are often at stake. The types of violation differ but the extent of urgency and seriousness call for changes. Out of many types, inhumane treatment, basic rights problem regarding both food and health crisis and freedom of association and speech are to be mainly discussed. The many human right issues are definitely related to the democratic transition in North Korea.

Considering such human right problems in North Korea, there were many attempts to address issues in international level. For instance, UN mandated Commission of Inquiry on Human Rights in the Democratic People's Republic of Korea. The committee held the recent public hearing in London, last 25th October 2013.[21)] Those who fled the North Korea deliver their stories regarding violation of human rights in North Korea. Not only organisations like UN but also numerous NGOs and human rights groups focus on this serious human rights infringement in North Korea.

The working conditions at the GIC have been a subject of debate. Jay Lefkowits, the United States special envoy on human rights in North Korea, has raised concerns about possible worker exploitation at the GIC, particularly the low salaries and their indirect payment.[22] Article 32 of the GIC Labour Law stipulates that South Korean companies shall pay wages to North Korean workers directly in cash. However, on North Korea's demand, South Korean companies remit worker salaries to the North Korean government, which in 2005 reportedly paid the workers an average of 6,300 North Korean won per month, or $42 using the official exchange rate of 150 North Korean won for on US dollar.

The GIC Labour Law does not establish the maximum work hours per week, but it stipulates that South Korean companies shall consult with worker's representatives prior to requesting workers to work overtime, and workers can refuse. North Korea' Labour Law, meanwhile, states that workers shall maintain a routine of eight hours of work, eight hours of study an eight hours of rest.[23] In spite of the rules, the Ministry of Unification told that North Korean workers at the GIC work eight hours per day and 48 hours per week, not including overtime. The average overtime for GIC workers in 2005 was reportedly 6.9 hours per week.

Although the GIC Labour Law addresses certain workers' right, many of the most fundamental rights are missing, therefore GIC Labour Law should be amended to meet international labour standards, and ensure the law is effectively enforced. Also North Korea should join the International Labour Organisation (ILO) and accede to the ILO's core treaties.[24] On the other hand, the country rejects the validity of universal human rights, even if it signed the universal declaration of human rights by joining the United Nations in 1991. North Korean claims that its 'human rights' concept should be equal to the UN Declaration of Human Rights and that it should be accepted internationally.[25]

The workers' rights criteria that Annex 22-B of the Korea-US FTA instructs the Committee to consider in determining whether to recommend free trade accord extension to North Korean outward processing zones are not sufficient to ensure respect for labour rights in those zones. The criteria are vague, weak, and fall far short of the new workers' right requirements in the main text of the FTA. As a result, they will allow the parties to permit the violation of the OPZ workers' basic rights under the agreement.[26]

Actually, Korea-US FTA could not raise the human right level of workers at the GIC. Likewise, it is anticipated that Korea-EU FTA relation could not influence the human right of the GIC workers either. To globalise the GIC with strengthening inter-Korean trade, developing human right condition of North Korean workers is essential and improvement in FTA level should be considered. Therefore, Korea and EU can and should do something for the purpose.

The European standard on the working conditions and human right issues will provide certain direction for the improvement of the level in the GIC. Even if the level is too high for the North Korean government to reach at the moment, the economic cooperation between the two parties with the consideration of the human right issues may make right progress. EU and Korea can do for the globalisation of the Complex with the human right issues in there based on the FTA relation. The cooperation will provide a gate for the North Korea to open.

IV. The Development issue in Korea and the FTA

1. Development issue in Korea

Korea eventually became the first nation changed the status from an aid recipient to a donor by joining Organization for Economic Cooperation and Development (OECD) Development Assistance Committee (DAC)[27] member via unprecedented growth process over the world in the past 60 years after overcoming the ruin of the Korean War.[28] The aid from international society made Korea in deep poverty morass enter in the line of donors. International society now expect for this small country to help their developing members.

The concept of Official Development Assistance (ODA) is the official assistance that advanced country provides give, loan, technical aid, and others to developing country or international organisation.[29] The world expects that Korea will play a role of leading donor in international society in the future, focused on the ODA field. The country as the DAC member is also striving to respond to the expectation and requirement of international society, keeping with many types of efforts in the field.

Korea promised to promote development cooperation corresponding to the international standards to perform the proper roles as an OECD DAC member by observing the rules and regulations decided by international society such as UN's Millennium Development Goals (MDGs) and OECD DAC's Rome Declaration, Paris Declaration, and Accra Agenda for Action.

Although Korea has tried to do many things in the international society, its experience as a donor is relatively short and the awareness on ODA is still needed to be improved. As far as the Korean government is concerned, ODA serves as a soft-power instrument in acquiring the status of an advanced country. The policy is linked with national interests and its objectives to obtain more influence in diplomacy, security and commerce and to secure natural resources. Approaches to and distributions of ODA are still highly donor and government-driven. It is not friendly with the concept of the partnership or ownership of recipients.[30)]

It is possible to criticise that the government lacks a coherent and consolidated system, especially regarding the implementation. The administration is characterised by competition between ministries and agencies. The ministry is responsible for loans and contributions to the multilateral development banks as well as for scaling-up ODA volume and aid budget allocations. It stresses national interests, economic cooperation and aid-for-oil in executing ODA. Therefore the criteria to select partner countries are based on bilateral economic relations and co-operation on investment, trade and natural resources.[31)]

As much as 75% of Korean ODA is tied, compared to an average of only 15% in the DAC in 2007. Despite there being a DAC recommendation on untying ODA to the least developed countries (LDCs) from 2001, the untied ratio of Korean ODA to the LDCs is only 20% compared to 98% for the other DAC countries excluding Korea. Nevertheless, the Korean government has recognised its obligation as a DAC member to untie aid and has therefore adopted a long-term roadmap of untying ODA to the level of 75% of total aid and 90% of aid to LDCs and heavily indebted poor countries by 2015.[32)]

Regarding the topics of the projects, Korea does not have programme approaches to achieve respect for human rights, sustainability, gender equity, and democratic ownership of the partner country. There are no overarching country assistance strategies agreed with partner countries based on high-level policy dialogue aid effectiveness principles or national plans and achievement of the MDGs. Korean ODA works are scattered across 30 partner countries via hundreds of individual projects chosen by Korean agencies and diplomats.[33)]

The networks with non-governmental organisations (NGOs) or civil society organisations (CSOs) are still weak point to the Korean ODA system. Furthermore, the ODA work lacks attention to ideas of local ownership, participation, empowerment, capacity building or sustainability. To improve the problems, the government must provide many stages and opportunities to discuss about the issue with the non-governmental players in the fields. The concept of Public-Private Partnership (PPP) can be available in this works.

2. Aid for Trade

Trade liberalisation is a controversial issue for developing countries. Majority of theoretical and empirical studies argue that trade can be a powerful engine to enhance economic development and poverty reduction.[34)] However, some countries were successful and others were not in reality. Namely, while developing countries are taking steps to liberalise their trade regimes, they cannot benefit from the opportunities offered by liberalisation.

The world trading system has caused more burden of trade liberalisation for developing countries. With the Uruguay Round, many developing countries became full participants of the multilateral trading system and agreed the single undertaking[35)] to submit schedules of concessions and commitments on market access, intellectual property rights and the service sector.[36)] Furthermore, developing countries, specifically the least developed ones, are not able to take advantage of increased market access due to internal obstacles to trade such as lack of knowledge, excessive bureaucracy, insufficient financing or poor infrastructure, weak productive capacity and low competitiveness.[37)]

Not only this background of trade issues for developing countries, but the international development community has experienced technical assistance for trade improvement in the name of ODA. In response to the worry of developing countries toward the WTO Agreement, new aid schemes in the form of Trade-Related Technical Assistance (TRTA) and Trade-Related Capacity Building (TRCB) have invented. At the 6th Ministerial Conference held in Hong Kong in 2005, the Ministerial Declaration endorsed the enhancement of the Integrated Framework and created a new WTO work programme on 'Aid for Trade.'

Since then, Aid for Trade has been considered as a new promising development tool for helping developing countries benefit under WTO agreements and expanding their trade.[38)] Thus, the definition of the concept has been broadened to include trade-related infrastructures, building productive capacity and trade-related adjustment. It is also focused on opening up the domestic economy to foreign trade, investment and competition, and integration into the world trading system. However, there are challenges of widening definition. The definitions of Aid for Trade categories are different among donor countries and between international organisations reflecting different priorities.[39)]

Aid for Trade mechanism must include monitoring capacity to ensure that the funds are being provided. Therefore, enlarged definition of Aid for Trade is the evidence of upgrading or developed concept compared to the past trade-related assistance. However, more careful management is necessary to achieve the objective of Aid for Trade regarding the broad concept and additional financial contribution.

The scope of Aid for Trade[40)] need to be defined because it reflects the diverse trade needs identified by countries and establishes a boundary between Aid for Trade and other development assistance. Projects and programmes should be considered as Aid for Trade if these activities have been identified as trade-related development priorities in the recipient country's national development strategies.

3. The up-grade of the Korean ODA to the North Korea with the FTA?

If the GIC is in the 'Globalisation policy' with international funds from the third countries for many reasons, rules are to be connected with other rules for the goals to provide global business standards. For example, the labour and environment level of the GIC would have a favourable influence on other judging standards such as recovering credibility of the North Korean government and stabilisation of the peninsula.

Another example can be made regarding the 'aid to the North' issue. South Korea may utilise its ODA funds for North Korea if they can regard the aid as a part of the ODA projects under the confirmed policy. In the case of establishing a supporting system to North Korea as ODA, the position of the South to the North would not same as other developing countries.[41] For example, if the inter-Korean economic cooperation can be done at the ODA level, the law on the Inter-Korean Cooperation Fund (IKCF) needs to be harmonised on the laws on the Korean ODA first.

Based on the concepts 'Development and Trade' or 'Aid for Trade,' ODA matters could be also related to the FTA issues. The assistance is an official action based on domestic and international laws. It also relies on economic trading actions of countries and enterprises which are the main subject of FTAs. The best use of FTA, the legal infrastructure, may make benefits for private and public fields. Therefore, it is considerable to harmonise some elements involved in FTA in ODA process with the reinforcement of the relevance of the ODA-FTA norm. If the FTA and the ODA policy of Korea are in harmony, it could make direct trade effects and economic profit.

Ultimately, the harmonisation of the ODA and the FTA policies and laws can increase benefit building and maintain the cooperation system with flexibility by economic, legal and other experts. Korea can anticipate the synergy by collaboration between their FTA policy and the inter-Korea economic cooperation, or the GIC project with the support of the ODA. Proper reformation of the inter-Korean and domestic laws which is suitable to the ODA-FTA policy and laws should be conducted in other fields as well. For example, the best way to give financial support to occupied enterprises in the GIC and to support small and medium sized businesses, and to support attracting overseas firm and foreign investment should be concretely discussed. On these issues, the Korea-EU FTA can provide new meanings as a legal infrastructure.

V. Concluding Remarks

In the part of the law, the concept of FTA is interesting. It is useful and important as a legal tool for international trade and economy. Therefore, legal researches are needed for the possible future FTAs to make the centre point of international economic law to members. This topic will also be important when they start designing the articles of the FTA and improving domestic laws of the members. Furthermore, FTAs assist in strengthening international partnerships with an economic interest combined with political motivation.

Many Korean FTAs including the Korea-EU FTA provide an opportunity to push for openness and respect for fundamental workers rights at the GIC. Although the OPZs rules in the Korea-EU FTA provide just small possibility of the special treatment, it is one of the few tools for North Korea to improve its economy and human right-related norms. The increased trade by the FTAs and globalisation policy on the Complex may produce to greater openness with the possibilities to push for the rights improvements in North Korea. It will be a small but important part of solutions for the human right and the democratic transition issues in the Korea.

However, there are still many problems to solve for the purpose. First of all, the labour and human right-related laws regarding the GIC must be amended or improved to the level of the international standards. At least, the existing provisions of the laws must be effectively enforced. Two Korean governments should make several opportunities to talk about the issue. The South Korean government also has some burden for the improvement with the GIC globalisation policy. The combination of the economic cooperation with the EU and the globalisation policy of the GIC may make a synergy effect for the solution to problems in the North Korea such as the human right issues.

Korea is considered to have advantages that it has development experience from one of the poorest countries to a donor within 60 years. As economy of most of developing countries has been, the majority of Korean economy was agriculture in the early phases of its development. Then it has developed manufacture industry and IT industry, which helps Korea to eradicate extreme poverty.[42)] Also, Korea experienced colonialism and severe war with the North Korea, which most of developing countries have also suffered. With developing its economy, it also achieved democracy though there were dictatorship and military regime until 1990s. All of these factors are familiar with developing countries' own experiences. Thus, there are common experiences in Korean and other developing partners.

If the ODA concept is accepted as a part of solutions on the Korean peninsula issues, the two Korean governments could anticipate unity and harmony on refinement and application of relative norms. Recently, there is an effort to reform the laws to make the Korean ODA policy efficient in the county. The inter-Korean cooperation and the GIC project are also considerable in this effort combining the ODA approach. If the main part of this support is up-grading the level of labour, environment and others to harmonise global standards, it would make another synergy with the above suggestion.

As a legal infrastructure, many Korean FTAs have many useful new meanings. They are not just for the economic benefits. These legal tools are also useful for the works of development or ODA issues, the management of the peace in Northeast Asian area and even the improvement of the North Korean human right environment. If the Korea-EU FTA has many provisions regarding the issues, we should find new implications in the legal infrastructure. These points can be related to many other Korean policies and legal factors.

1) Bong-chul, Kim, *Understanding Free Trade Agreement* (Korea Corporate Legal Affairs Association, 2007), pp.155-156.

2) European Commission, "EU-South Korea Free Trade Agreement: A Quick Reading Guide, October 2010", http://trade.ec.europa.eu/doclib/docs/2009/october/tradoc_145203.pdf, 6/12/2013, p. 2.

3) Act on the Investigation of Unfair International Trade Practices and Remedy against Injury to Industry.

4) Safeguard Measures by Free Trade Agreements with Foreign States.

5) Abatement of Implementation of Safeguard Measures against FTA Counterparts.

6) Trade Damage Support Measures on Increase in Import of Special Goods following FTA.

7) Cooperation with Foreign State after FTA.

8) Park Chang-Hyun, *The Role of the National Assembly in the Process of Trade Negotiation*, Korea Legislation Research Institute, 2008, pp. 177-178.

9) Choi, Won Mok, "How to Amend Domestic Laws on the South-North Korean Relationship, pursuant to the Conclusion of FTAs – Focusing on the scope of application clauses of FTAs and the issue of rules of origin of products manufactured in the Kae-Sung Industrial Complex." *Korea Legislation Research Institute* (2008): 30-31.

10) Cho, Myung-Chul and others, "Strategies for Promoting Exports of Companies in Gaeseong Industrial Complex," *Korea Institute for International Economic Policy* (2005): 16-27.

11) See Kaesong Industrial District Management Committee [http://www.kidmac.com].

12) Lim, Eul-chul, *Kaesong Industrial Complex History Pending Issues, and Outlook*, (Seoul: Haenum Publishing Company, 2006), 172.

13) Cho, Bong-hyun, "Kaesong Industrial Complex Development and Inter-Korean Relations," *KDI Review of the North Korean Economy*, (2011).

14) "NK denies delegation entry to Gaeseong," *Korea Times*, April 17, 2013.

15) "Political parties oppose power cut off to Gaeseong," *Korea Times*, May 1, 2013.

16) "Koeas begin 5th round of talks on Kaesong park normalization," *Koreatimes*, July 22, 2013.

17) "Kaesong industrial park talks end without agreement," *Maeil Business Newspaper*, July 16, 2013.

18) "Two Koreas will guarantee unconditional reoperation come to agreement on Kaesong," *ZD Net Korea*, August 15, 2013.

19) However, considering the economic stages of the ASEAN countries, the preferential treatment of the GIC-produced goods shall end from the date of the entry into force.

20) Mark E. Manyin and others, "Imports from North Korea: Existing Rules, Implications of the KORUS FTA, and the Kaesong Industrial Complex", *CRS Report for Congress, The US Congressional Research Service 7-5700*, (2011): 15.

21) Official High Commissioner for Human Rights (OHCHR). *UN human rights investigators on DPRK hear shocking testimonies in London*. 25-10-2013. http://www.ohchr.org/EN/NewsEvents/Pages/DisplayNews.aspx?NewsID=13904&LangID=E (Accessed 26-10-2013)

22) Jay Lefkowitz, "Freedom for all Koreans," *The Wall Street Journal*, April 28, 2006

23) North Korean Labour Law, art.33.

24) North Korea: Workers' Rights and the Kaesong Industrial Complex, Human Rights Watch, October, 2006

25) "Kaesong industrial zone will not change much in North Korea", Press

release by *Religion und Politik* on 32nd German Oriental Studies Conference (Deutscher Orientalistentag, DOT) at the University of Münster, September 2013.

25) The US-Korea Free Trade Agreement Annex 22-B: A Missed Opportunity on Workers' Rights in North Korea, Human Rights Watch, August 2007.

27) The OECD Development Assistance Committee (DAC) is a unique international forum of many of the largest funders of aid, including 24 members. The World Bank, IMF and UNDP participate as observers. The DAC's to countries beyond its members who are making growing contributions to development co-operation. The DAC became part of the OECD by Ministerial Resolution on 23 July 1961. (OECD DAC, http://www.oecd.org/document/1/0,3746,en_2649_33721_46662849_1_1_1_1,00.html).

28) KOICA, "Understanding International Development Cooperation", 2008, pp.394-395.

29) ODA KOREA, [http://www.odakorea.go.kr/index.jsp], 2013. 7. 29.

30) Lee Tae Joo, "Korea Joins the Big League with a Donor-centric Approach" in Alex Wilks (eds), Aid and Development Effectiveness: Towards Human Rights, Social Justice and Democracy, Reality of Aid 2010 report (The Reality of Aid Management Committee), IBON Books, Philippines, 2010, p. 234.

31) *Ibid.*

32) *Ibid.*

33) *Ibid.*

34) Winters, A., McCulloch, N. and Mckay, A. 2004. Trade Liberalization and Poverty: The Evidence So Far. *Journal of Economic Literature*, 42(1), pp 72-115.

35) Single undertaking approach means members cannot selectively apply the range of agreements but they have to accept or refuse

the whole package. Namely, single undertaking approach presents the very opposite of the GATT approach that had evolved by the time of the Tokyo Round. Also, it includes the dispute settlement understanding, the substantive agreements on goods, services, investment measures and intellectual property rights.

36) OECD. 2006. Aid for Trade: making it effective. *Organization for Economic Co-operation and Developemt*, Paris.

37) Hoekman, B. and Nicita, A. 2010. Assessing the Doha Round: Market Access, Transactions Costs and Aid for Trade Facilitation. *Journal of International trade & Economic Development*, 19(1), pp 65-79.

38) OECD. 2006. Aid for Trade: making it effective. *Organization for Economic Co-operation and Developemt*, Paris; Helble, M., Mann, C and Wilson J.S. 2009. Aid for Trade Facilitation. *Policy Research Working Paper Series*, World Bank.

39) IMF and World Bank. 2007. Aid for Trade: Harnessing Globalization for Development, Washington, DC, August.

40) WTO, Recommendations of the Task Force on Aid for Trade https://docs.wto.org/dol2fe/Pages/FE_Search/FE_S_S009-1.aspx?language=E&CatalogueIdList=69598,58039,64435,58619,55641,58379,51994,52316,51741,54208&CurrentCatalogueIdIndex=5&FullTextSearch=

41) However, when an OECD DAC inspectorate visited Seoul in 2008 and asked if South Korea was willing to include its assistance to North Korea in the ODA, the South Korean authority was unable to provide a definite answer. This ambiguous situation remains unresolved and it must be politically determined [Chung, Sang Hwa, "A Prospect for Inter-Korean Economic Development Cooperation: Utilizing ODA to Promote Multilateral Forestation Projects," *International Journal of Korean Unification Studies*, Vol.21, No.2 (2012): 125].

42) IDCC, (2010), The Mid-term ODA Policy for 2011-2015.

This Chapter is based on author's article in Journal of European Union Studies (Vol. 37, 2014) titled *Legal response to the Korea-EU FTA: Is it possible to use the law for other purposes?*

KOREAN
FTA
POLICY AND LAW

Chapter 4.
The Trade Remedy Issues in the Korea-EU FTA

The Trade Remedy Issues in the Korea-EU FTA

Joonpye Lee and Hyelim Lee

I. Introduction

Korea and the EU have developed relations for more than 50 years officially. The relations between the two partners have various aspects, such as on political, cultural, economic, security matters. Especially, economic and trade cooperation continue to show high possibilities of development. Particularly, the trade between Korea and the EU has been developed rapidly after launching the WTO. Due to the global economic crisis, the trade growth of the two partners was slow,[1] however, it started to grow again in 2010.[2]

The conclusion of two bilateral agreements has resulted in developed relations. The first one is the Agreement on Co-operation and Mutual Administrative Assistance in Customs Matters which was signed on 13 May 1997 and the second one is the Framework Agreement for Trade and Co-operation which was enacted on 1 April 2001.[3)] Furthermore, In April 2007, Korea and the EU started negotiating for a bilateral FTA and while having the EU-Republic of Korea Summit in Brussels, the FTA was signed on 6 October 2010[4)] and entered into force on 1 July 2011.

European Commission described the FTA as "the most ambitious free trade agreement ever negotiated by the EU and the first with a partner country in Asia. Import duties are to be eliminated on nearly all products, 98.7% of duties in terms of trade value will be eliminated within five years...".[5)] Thus, as duties on all goods will practically be removed, there must be Non-Tariff Barriers (NTBs) which nevertheless could make the trade between two partners more difficult.

Since 1947, the General Agreement on Tariffs and Trade (GATT) and subsequent WTO accords to have lower tariff rates among the member countries,[6)] the countries may prefer to protect their domestic industries through the other way as NTBs rather than imposing tariffs. International trade raises profit from the investment and exportation so it leads to motivate economic growth through economies of scale, but it also could cause serious injury to the domestic goods which have no comparative advantage. Therefore, each country imposes certain measures or legal controls to protect its domestic industry excluded from the way of tariffs under the barriers.

Accordingly, this chapter attempts to find out what might be obstacles as NTBs to make the countries adapt a defensive posture and protect their domestic industry, and focus on the trade remedy issues in the Korea-EU FTA. After the analysis of the provisions on the trade remedy, it will suggest several points for better regulation of their trade.

II. Trade Remedy System in Korea and the EU

1. Trade Remedy System in Korea

The principal laws of trade remedy system in Korea are under the Act on the Investigation of Unfair International Trade Practices and Remedy against Injury to Industry (Trade Remedy Act) and the Customs Act. The Trade Remedy Act is the first comprehensive trade remedy law which covers the investigation of unfair trade activities, safeguard actions, investigation of injury to a given industry competitiveness, and the organization and function of the Korea Trade Commission (KTC).[7]

However, Article 23 (investigations of Injury to Industry Caused by Dumping, etc.) and Article 24 (Investigations of Injury to Industry Caused by Subsidies, etc.) of the Trade Remedy Act show that all of the substantive and procedural rules on anti-dumping and countervailing measures "shall be made in accordance with Articles 51 through 56 of the Customs Act" and "shall be made in accordance with Articles 57 through 62 of the Customs Act" respectively.[8] Therefore, one can say that Customs Act is the primary source of the trade remedy measures in Korea. Fundamentally, the Customs Act with the Foreign Trade Act (enacted on 31 December 1986 as Act No. 3895) had been the principle laws of foreign trade in Korea before the Trade Remedy Act was enacted.[9]

The KTC carries out the administration of the measures and investigates and determines whether imports are dumped or subsidized and whether they cause or threaten to cause injury to the domestic industry under the Ministry of Knowledge Economy (MKE). KTC investigations find out whether imports have cause or threatened to cause "serious" injury to domestic industry under emergency safeguard provisions. The decision of imposing on anti-dumping and countervailing duties is taken by the Ministry of Strategy and Finance (MOSF).[10]

Korea's WTO notification states that "parts of the Customs Act and its sub regulations on anti-dumping measures were revised and have been in force since March 2011."[11] Generally, principle laws of trade remedy in Korea has been amended continuously in order to respect international standards accordance with the WTO system and to make an effort not to deviate from that framework is still ongoing. However, to have a quick response to rapid change of the WTO and international community standards due to such as FTAs still remain to be worked out for adapting the various change of trade environment.

2. Trade Remedy System in the EU

The European Commission oversees the use of trade defence instruments, which are called contingency measures, and these measures are part of the Common Commerce Policy (CCP). When EU's industries complain with the Commission, it leads to initiate an investigation. If the investigation determines whether there is dumping or subsidies and whether they cause injury to the EU's industries, the Commission may suggest contingency measures to the Council. Trade defence instruments may be used in accordance with WTO agreements, to against practice of unfair trade by other countries. They are composed as follow:[12)]

- *Anti-dumping measures: used to counter dumping, which occurs when manufacturers from a non-EU country sell goods in the EU below the sales price in their domestic market or below the cost of production–this is the most frequent trade distorting practice.*
- *Anti-subsidy measures: used to combat subsidies, which help to reduce production costs from abroad or cut the price of EU exports, with the consequence of distorting trade.*
- *Safeguards: the WTO allows a country to temporarily restrict imports of a product if its domestic industry is seriously injured by a surge in imports.*

In March 2011, the adoption of contingency measures to the comitology rules came into effect. It requires a positive opinion by Qualified Majority Voting (QMA) of a committee which made up of member State representatives.[13)]

In addition, Regulation No. 1225/2009 which is basic anti-dumping regulations was revised twice in September and December 2012 considering the rulings of the WTO Dispute Settlement Body and the European Court of Justice. In October 2011, the Commission undertook a plan to improve trade defence instrument. This initiative includes the anti-dumping and countervailing instrument in order to use efficiency and effectively. However, safeguards are excluded due to the difference procedure to impose from the anti-dumping and countervailing instruments.[14)]

As can be understood from here that the EU has exclusive power to the trade defence. It means that the laws and actions of individual member states are integrated to the EU-wide laws and actions.[15)] Therefore, when a member state of the EU complains with Commission and if it is inappropriate to the EU's standards of trade defence system, they rejected by the EU at an EU level.

3. Trend of the trade remedies in Korea and the EU

According to the WTO Secretariat, countries have been using more anti-dumping measures compared to countervailing duties or safeguard measures among the trade remedy measures in general.[16] The notifications on safeguards during the period from 01 January 1995 to 30 April 2013, there are not many actions used typically, compared to the anti-dumping measures. In total, the EU had 3 safeguard measures in force while Korea had 2 safeguard measures.[17] However, WTO members impose the most anti-dumping measures unlike the safeguard measures, since the establishment of the WTO in 1995. During the period from 01 January 1995 to 31 December 2013, the EU have been imposed 297 anti-dumping measures while Korea has imposed 77 measures on anti-dumping.[18] Moreover, interestingly, there have been no countervailing duty cases in Korea, while 33 countervailing measures have been imposed by the EU during the period from 01 January 1995 to 31 December 2013.[19]

Therefore, it is obvious that Korea and the EU also have been imposing anti-dumping measures significantly more than the safeguard measures and the countervailing measures. Its reason is that WTO anti-dumping rules do not demand to compensate the affected countries for tariff reductions from the imposing country, and they do not require to allow the affected countries to retaliate. This is why countries can impose anti-dumping duties without fear.[20]

In summary, Korea and the EU also have been using more anti-dumping measures compared to the rest of the trade remedies. In addition, the EU is the third anti-dumping user during the period from 1995 to 2012 by initiations, and Korea is the second in the targets of anti-dumping investigation at the same period. Therefore, anti-dumping measures might be an obstacle between the two partners.

On the other hand, there is a case that Hyundai and Kia accused of dumping practices by French minister after the FTA implementation which shows confirming anti-dumping is not always possible. For example, France requested to the Commission to monitor on Korean car imports by explaining the reason of losing sales of their domestic automaker because of sharing their car market with Korean cars especially from Hyundai and Kia companies. In conclusion, the European Commission refused the request from France to introduce prior surveillance.

It implies that France did not have enough reasons to prove dumping from Korean cars. Even though when countries request application for investigation or impose anti-dumping duties without any fear of retaliation, it is possible to learn from this case that confirming anti-dumping decision needs to meet certain requirements.

III. Trade Remedy Measures in the Korea-EU FTA

1. Trade Remedy Rules in Chapter Three of the Korea-EU FTA

As FTAs have been proliferating through the open economy, countries want to protect their domestic industry with NTBs in contrast with the using tariffs. Korea started being interested in Regional Trade Agreements (RTAs)[21] in 1997, after the Asian financial crisis, when they realized about RTA's importance and decided to use them to overcome the economic and financial crisis.[22] So far, Korea has built the FTA relations with Chile, Singapore, EFTA, ASEAN, India, EU, Peru, the US and Turkey respectively. Therefore, the importance of trade remedy measures is being emphasized.

In the Korea-EU FTA, the agreement comprises fifteen Chapters, several annexes and appendixes, three protocols and four understandings. Among them, Chapter Three on trade remedies consists of five sections with sixteen articles. Section A in this chapter is on bilateral safeguard measures which includes conditions and limitations, provision measures, and procedures of compensation. Section B and C provide agricultural safeguard measures and global safeguard measures respectively, and Section D sets out the rules for anti-dumping and countervailing duties. Section E is for working group on trade remedy cooperation in this FTA.

<The Trade Remedy Provisions on the Korea-EU FTA>

Section	Article	Title
Section A Bilateral Safeguard Measures	Article 3.1	Application of a Bilateral Safeguard Measure
	Article 3.2	Conditions and Limitations
	Article 3.3	Provision Measures
	Article 3.4	Compensation
	Article 3.5	Definitions
Section B Agricultural Safeguard Measures	Article 3.6	Agricultural Safeguard Measures
Section C Global Safeguard Measures	Article 3.7	Global Safeguard Measures
Section D Anti-Dumping and Countervailing Duties	Article 3.8	Anti-dumping and Countervailing Duties
	Article 3.9	Notification
	Article 3.10	Consideration of Public Interests
	Article 3.11	Investigation after Termination Resulting from a Review
	Article 3.12	Cumulative Assessment
	Article 3.13	De-minimis Standard Applicable to Review
	Article 3.14	Lesser Duty Rule
	Article 3.15	Dispute Settlement
Section E Institutional Provisions	Article 3.16	Working Group on Trade Remedy Cooperation

Source: Ministry of Trade, Industry & Energy (MOTIE)

2. Provisions on the Korea-EU FTA

- Provisions on Safeguard Measures of the FTA

According to the Article 3.1, bilateral safeguard measures can be used when increased imported goods cause or threaten to cause serious injury to a domestic industry of the Parties as a result of the reduction or elimination of a custom duty through this Agreement. However, according to the Article 3.2, Each Party may not apply a bilateral safeguard measure for a period exceeding two years, "except that the period may be extended by up to two years" and the "total period of application of a safeguard measures, including the period of initial application and any extension thereof, shall not exceed four years."

In addition, when there is clear evidence that imported goods cause serious damage to a domestic industry of both parties, "a Party may apply a bilateral safeguard measure on a provisional basis pursuant to a preliminary determination" which shall not exceed 200 days in the FTA in accordance with the Article 3.3. Moreover, the transition period of bilateral safeguard measures is "until 10 years from the date of completion of tariff reduction or elimination, as the case may be for each good," accordance with the Article 3.5.

Also, the Article 3.4 states that when a Party is applying a bilateral safeguard measures, it must provide an opportunity to consult with the other Party no later than 30 days after its application, in order to accord a compensation in the form of concessions which have "substantially trade effects or equivalent to the value of the additional duties expected to result from the safeguard measure."

Furthermore, when the sensitive "agricultural goods listed in the Schedule included in Annex 3" are imported "in any year exceeds a trigger level as set out in its Schedule included in Annex 3," the agricultural safeguard measures are automatically imposed. However, Party may not apply these measures with a bilateral safeguard measure.

About the global safeguard measures, the Parties can take safeguard measures "under Article XIX of GATT 1994 and the Agreement on Safeguards," according to the Article 3.7. However, like the agricultural safeguard measures, these global safeguard measures cannot apply with a bilateral safeguard measure at the same time.

So far, the characteristics of the provisions on safeguard measures of the Korea-EU FTA are examined. As referred to earlier, agricultural safeguard measures and global safeguard measures cannot be used with bilateral safeguard measures at the same time. In other words, it can be said that the bilateral safeguard measures are the main provisions and it affects materially to the both parties in the FTA.

- Provisions on Anti-dumping and Countervailing Duties of the FTA

In the Korea-EU FTA, Article 3.8 contains the general provisions regarding anti-dumping and countervailing duties, which provide for compliance with Article VI of GATT 1994, the WTO Anti-dumping Agreement, and the Agreement on Subsidies and Countervailing Measures. According to the Article 3.9 in the FTA, "after receipt by a Party's competent authorities of a properly documented anti-dumping application with respect to imports from the other Party," the Party has to offer "written notification to the other Party of its receipt of the application" no later than 15 days before the investigation has started.

On the other hand, Article 5.5 of the Anti-dumping Agreement states that "after receipt of a properly documented application and before proceeding to initiate an investigation, the authorities shall notify the government of the exporting Member concerned." That is to say, the WTO rules have only obligation to notify, nevertheless, the FTA specifies period that the notification must be no later than 15 days.

The FTA also has provision for consideration of public interest. Before the Parties imposing an anti-dumping or countervailing duty, they "shall endeavour to consider the public interests" However, the WTO Anti-dumping Agreement doesn't have regulation related to the public interest.

In addition, Article 3.12 of the FTA prescribes an obligation to the Parties, indicating that a Party shall examine "whether the cumulative assessment of the effect of the imports of the other Party is appropriate" when the imports coming from more than on country are simultaneously subject to investigation. Nevertheless, according to the Article 3.3 of the WTO Anti-dumping Agreement, the authorities may cumulatively assess the effects of this kind of imports in the same situations provided in the FTA, therefore, being less strict as it does not contain an obligation.

Moreover, according to the Article 3.13 of the FTA, "any measures subject to REVIEW pursuant to Article 11 of the Anti-dumping Agreement shall be terminated where it is determined that the likely recurring dumping margin is less than the de-minimis threshold set out in Article 5.8 of the Anti-dumping Agreement," on the other hand, de-minimis is applicable to original investigation, according to the Article 5.8 of the WTO rules. However, it doesn't really include specific statements which shall makes applicable to review.

Furthermore, the FTA includes Lesser Duty Rules that a Party "should decide to impose an anti-dumping or countervailing duty, the amount of such duty shall not exceed the margin of dumping or countervailable subsidies, and it should be less than the margin if such lesser duty would be adequate to remove the injury to the domestic industry. On the other hand, according to the Article 9.1 of WTO Anti-dumping Agreement and the Article 19.2 of the Agreement on Subsidies and Countervailing Measures, "it is DESIRABLE that the imposition be permissive … if such lesser duty would be adequate to…" It means it doesn't have obligatory application.

3. The FTA provisions – From International Laws to Domestic Laws

In the Korea-EU FTA, trade remedy rules contain three different kinds of provisions on safeguard measures which are the bilateral safeguard measures, the agricultural safeguard measures, and the global safeguard measures, with anti-dumping and countervailing duties also.

However, there are differences in the period for the each provision in the Korean major FTAs to the safeguard measures compared to the FTA between Korea and the EU. For instance, in the Korea-EU FTA, both parties cannot take a bilateral safeguard measure for a period exceeding two year as mentioned before, one year in the Korea-EFTA FTA[23) regarding bilateral safeguard measures, three years in the Korea-ASEAN FTA[24) regarding safeguard measures, and two years in the Korea-US FTA[25) regarding safeguard measures.

Also, except that possible extension period does not exceed two years in the Korea-EU FTA, one year in the Korea-ASEAN FTA and the Korea-US FTA. In addition, the period of application of a safeguard measures cannot exceed four years, three years in the Korea-EFTA FTA, three years in the Korea-US FTA. Moreover, In the Korea-EU FTA, the duration of any provisional measures must be terminated within 200 days, likewise the Korea-EFTA FTA and the Korea-US FTA.

Another example of the difference period is the transition period. As stated before, In the Korea-EU FTA, transition period is "until 10 years from the date of completion of tariff reduction or elimination," unlike the fact that in the Korea-US FTA, transition period is "ten-year period following the date when this Agreement enters into force, except that for any good for which the Schedule to Annex 2-B (Tariff Elimination) of the Party applying the safeguard measure provides for the Party to eliminate its tariffs on the good over a period of more than ten years."

Therefore, it can be found that there is little difference of period, even though they seem to have similar provisions in safeguard measures. Also, it is meaningful that the Korea-EU FTA has a section on agricultural safeguard measures to protect some sensitive agricultural products of each party. In addition, both parties provide an institutional strategy to mitigate anti-dumping and countervailing duties as barriers by complying more stringent regulations than the WTO legislation.

FTAs can regulate international relations as international laws. At the same time, they are able to be used as domestic laws. According to the Korean legal system, certain Korean FTAs can be directly applied to the Korean society and many Korean domestic rules have been changed for the FTA regulations.

As mentioned earlier, Customs law and the Law on the Inspection of Unfair Trade Act and Trade Remedies (Act on the Investigation of Unfair International Trade Practices and Remedy against Injury to Industry) are major substantive laws on the trade remedy issue. Based on the concept of the general rules, there are some special provisions regarding the Korean FTAs. For example, Article 22-3 (Safeguard Measures by Free Trade Agreements with Foreign States), 22-4 (Abatement of Implementation of Safeguard Measures against FTA Counterparts), 22-5 (Trade Damage Support Measures on Increase in Import of Special Goods following FTA) and 22-6 (Cooperation with Foreign State after FTA) of the Inspection of Unfair Trade Act and Trade Remedies make some exception with the FTAs. Furthermore, 'Act on Special Cases of the Custom Act for the Implementation of Free Trade Agreements' also provides special rules on the Korean FTA.[26)]

IV. Concluding Remarks

National trade policies have been adopting trade remedies to secure domestic industries due to the liberalization of trade, such as FTAs. Therefore, it is significantly important to know about other countries' trade remedies in order to prepare or respond to the trade defence system of other parties. Thus, this chapter dealt with the trade remedy system in Korea and the EU and trade remedy measures in the Korea-EU FTA. Consequently, it was confirmed that the rules of trade barriers were softened compared to the other major Korean FTAs.

However, Korea and the EU are not an exception to use more anti-dumping measures than safeguard and countervailing measures as tendency to use of the trade remedies in general, it is obvious that the anti-dumping is an obstacle between Korea and the EU as well. In addition, Korea faced the second largest number of anti-dumping lawsuits in 2012 after the China, while the EU was the fourth in the anti-dumping top users by initiations in 2012. With these reasons, Korea needs to develop the response norm and policy in order to adapt to new and continually changing circumstances of trade policy, while it does close monitoring to the EU's policy.

Moreover, it needs to release more information and to communicate between the businesses, parties, and the authorities in accordance with the Korea-EU FTA. In particular, Korea needs to strengthen information gathering on trade remedy measures through industrial and sectorial analysis for constructing an integrated database. Also, Korea should increase its efforts to settle the trade remedy measures through the utilization of the FTA between Korea and the EU in order to reinforce support for Small and Medium-sized Enterprise (SME)'s.

Korea and the EU are required to revise domestic rules for the FTA. It is also necessary for 28 member states to amend the domestic rules for the EU's mutual regulations. In addition, as both parties provide an institutional strategy to mitigate anti-dumping and countervailing duties as barriers by complying more stringent regulations than WTO legislation, trade remedy must be a 'remedy', not a 'barrier' to the trade, thus watching regulation and restriction is also needed to avoid 'unfair trade'. Furthermore, through bilateral cooperation, Korea and the EU need to make a joint effort to develop WTO criteria in the international community.

1) Delegation of the European Union to the Republic of Korea, *European Union-South Korea: Trade and investment relations*, 2013. p. 2.

2) The EU exported goods worth €32.4 billion and services worth €7.5 billion to Korea in 2011. Indeed, the EU is the second largest source of imports to Korea, only after China. See, James Harrison, *The European Union and South Korea: The Legal Framework for Strengthening Trade*, Economic and Political Relations, Edinburgh University Press Ltd, 2014, p. 149.

3) Alex Marx et al., "EU-Korea Relations in a Changing World", Leuven Centre for Global Governance Studies, 2013, p. 3.

4) *Ibid.*, p. 5.

5) European Commission, *The EU-Korea Free Trade Agreement in practice*, 2011, p. 3.

6) Krugman R. Paul and Obstfelf Maurice and Melitz J. Marc, *International Economics, Theory&Policy (9th Edition)*, Pearson Education Limited, 2012, pp. 269-270.

7) Seungwha Chang and Wonmog Choi, *Trade Law and Regulation in Korea*, Edward Elgar Publishing Limited, 2011, p. 39.

8) Korea Trade Commission, "Law and Decrees", http://www.ktc.go.kr/en/pro/pro_law_act.jsp, 17/8/2014.

9) Seungwha Chang and Wonmog Choi, *op. cit.*,, p. 40.

10) WTO, "Trade policy review", The Secretariat – Republic of Korea, 2012, p. 65.

11) *Ibid.*

12) Christopher Hill and Michael Smith, *International Relations and the European Union*, Oxford University Press, 2011, p. 283.

13) WTO, "Trade Policy review", The Secretariat – European Union, 2013, p. 52.

14) *Ibid.*, p. 53.

15) European Commission, "Enlargement: Impact on Trade Defence", http://trade.ec.europa.eu/doclib/docs/2013/march/tradoc_150782.pdf, 20/8/2014.

16) Seungrae Lee, "Recent Trends in Trade Remedies and Its Implications on Korea", Korea Institute for International Economic Policy, October 2013, p. 2.

17) WTO, "Safeguard Measures by Reporting Member", http://www.wto.org/english/tratop_e/safeg_e/SG-Measures_By_Reporting_Member.pdf, 21/8/2014.

18) WTO, "Anti-dumping Measures: By Reporting Member", http://www.wto.org/english/tratop_e/adp_e/AD_MeasuresByRepMem.pdf, 21/8/2014.

19) WTO, "Countervailing Measures: By Reporting Member", http://www.wto.org/english/tratop_e/scm_e/CV_MeasuresByRepMem.pdf, 21/8/2014.

20) Thomas J. Prusa, "Anti-dumping: A Growing Problem in International Trade", *The World Economy*, Vol. 28, No. 5 (May 2005), p. 697.

21) In the age of globalization, levying duties on imported and exported goods have been progressively lowered regarding open economy through the Free Trade Agreement (FTA), Customs Union (CU), and Common Market (CM) as Regional Trade Agreements (RTAs) which support World Trade Organization (WTO)'s multilateral system.

22) Bongchul Kim, *Trade Remedy Regulations in Regional Trade Agreements: Proposals on the provisions of the Northeast Asian FTA*, Lambert Academic Publishing, 2009, p. 156.

23) Korea-EFTA FTA: Article 2.11.

24) Korea-ASEAN FTA: Article 9.

25) Korea-US FTA: Article 10.2.

26) Bongchul Kim, "Legal response to the Korea-EU FTA: Is it possible to use the law for other purposes?", *Journal of European Union Studies*, Vol. 37, (June 2014), p. 173.

This Chapter is based on authors' article in Journal of European Union Studies (Vol. 38, 2014) titled *New Types of Trade Barriers?: The Trade Remedy Issues in the Korea-EU FTA.*

KOREAN FTA

POLICY AND LAW

Authors

Authors

- *Bongchul Kim* is a professor in International Economic and Trade Law at Hankuk University of Foreign Studies (HUFS). He holds a PhD in Law at King's College London (University of London) with Overseas Research Scholarships (ORS) by the UK government. Professor Kim also holds Bachelor and Master Degrees of Law at HUFS.

- *Ho Kim* is a Lecturer at HUFS. He holds a SJD at American University (Washington College of Law) and LLM at University of Minnesota Law School. Dr. Kim also holds Bachelor and Master Degrees of Law at HUFS.

- *Joonpyo Lee* is a Lecturer at HUFS. He holds a PhD, Master and Bachelor degrees in Law at HUFS. Currently, he has been delivering a research project on international issues of the Greater Mekong Subregion's Countries at Seoul National University.

- *Hyelim Lee* is a PhD Candidate at HUFS on International Relations. She holds a Master degree in EU Studies from Graduate School of International and Area Studies (GSIAS) at HUFS. She has been delivering several research projects on international issues, especially regarding the EU area.